C-1644 CAREER EXAMINATION SERIES

This is your
PASSBOOK for...

Workers' Compensation Examiner

Test Preparation Study Guide
Questions & Answers

COPYRIGHT NOTICE

This book is SOLELY intended for, is sold ONLY to, and its use is RESTRICTED to individual, bona fide applicants or candidates who qualify by virtue of having seriously filed applications for appropriate license, certificate, professional and/or promotional advancement, higher school matriculation, scholarship, or other legitimate requirements of education and/or governmental authorities.

This book is NOT intended for use, class instruction, tutoring, training, duplication, copying, reprinting, excerption, or adaptation, etc., by:

1) Other publishers
2) Proprietors and/or Instructors of "Coaching" and/or Preparatory Courses
3) Personnel and/or Training Divisions of commercial, industrial, and governmental organizations
4) Schools, colleges, or universities and/or their departments and staffs, including teachers and other personnel
5) Testing Agencies or Bureaus
6) Study groups which seek by the purchase of a single volume to copy and/or duplicate and/or adapt this material for use by the group as a whole without having purchased individual volumes for each of the members of the group
7) Et al.

Such persons would be in violation of appropriate Federal and State statutes.

PROVISION OF LICENSING AGREEMENTS – Recognized educational, commercial, industrial, and governmental institutions and organizations, and others legitimately engaged in educational pursuits, including training, testing, and measurement activities, may address request for a licensing agreement to the copyright owners, who will determine whether, and under what conditions, including fees and charges, the materials in this book may be used them. In other words, a licensing facility exists for the legitimate use of the material in this book on other than an individual basis. However, it is asseverated and affirmed here that the material in this book CANNOT be used without the receipt of the express permission of such a licensing agreement from the Publishers. Inquiries re licensing should be addressed to the company, attention rights and permissions department.

All rights reserved, including the right of reproduction in whole or in part, in any form or by any means, electronic or mechanical, including photocopying, recording, or by any information storage and retrieval system, without permission in writing from the Publisher.

Copyright © 2025 by
National Learning Corporation

212 Michael Drive, Syosset, NY 11791
(516) 921-8888 • www.passbooks.com
E-mail: info@passbooks.com

PASSBOOK® SERIES

THE *PASSBOOK® SERIES* has been created to prepare applicants and candidates for the ultimate academic battlefield – the examination room.

At some time in our lives, each and every one of us may be required to take an examination – for validation, matriculation, admission, qualification, registration, certification, or licensure.

Based on the assumption that every applicant or candidate has met the basic formal educational standards, has taken the required number of courses, and read the necessary texts, the *PASSBOOK® SERIES* furnishes the one special preparation which may assure passing with confidence, instead of failing with insecurity. Examination questions – together with answers – are furnished as the basic vehicle for study so that the mysteries of the examination and its compounding difficulties may be eliminated or diminished by a sure method.

This book is meant to help you pass your examination provided that you qualify and are serious in your objective.

The entire field is reviewed through the huge store of content information which is succinctly presented through a provocative and challenging approach – the question-and-answer method.

A climate of success is established by furnishing the correct answers at the end of each test.

You soon learn to recognize types of questions, forms of questions, and patterns of questioning. You may even begin to anticipate expected outcomes.

You perceive that many questions are repeated or adapted so that you can gain acute insights, which may enable you to score many sure points.

You learn how to confront new questions, or types of questions, and to attack them confidently and work out the correct answers.

You note objectives and emphases, and recognize pitfalls and dangers, so that you may make positive educational adjustments.

Moreover, you are kept fully informed in relation to new concepts, methods, practices, and directions in the field.

You discover that you are actually taking the examination all the time: you are preparing for the examination by "taking" an examination, not by reading extraneous and/or supererogatory textbooks.

In short, this PASSBOOK®, used directedly, should be an important factor in helping you to pass your test.

WORKERS' COMPENSATION EXAMINER

DUTIES
Workers' Compensation Examiners, under supervision, with some latitude for independent action or decision, perform investigation and claim-processing tasks related to workers' compensation cases, and perform related work.

Examine, evaluate and develop workers' compensation, disability benefits and volunteer firefighter's benefit claims. You would also evaluate accident, disability and medical reports; secure necessary forms and documents for development of cases; and prepare and process awards based on Referee or Board decisions.

EXAMPLES OF TYPICAL TASKS
Reviewing accident reports and other documents related to incoming claims to determine workers' compensation coverage; setting up computer files, entering information into the computer and updating computer records; contacting City agency staff to make inquiries regarding claims; returning incomplete claims to the appropriate party for additional information; gathering information from case files or computer records and preparing written material and forms for distribution; responding to telephone inquiries from claimants and their attorneys and physicians; scheduling independent medical examinations to determine entitlement to workers' compensation benefits; making inquiries about medical background of claimants; reviewing pending cases for possible third-party coverage; preparing recommendation for compensation; and processing payments for medical treatment. Perform related work.

SCOPE OF THE EXAMINATION
The written test will cover knowledge, skills and abilities in such areas as:

1. Reading and understanding reports, rules and regulations, and other materials based on the Workers' Compensation Law;
2. Applying written narrative and tabular material related to the Workers' Compensation Law, regulations and/or administrative determinations in the processing and computing of benefit awards;
3. Preparing various written materials and forms, including knowledge of grammar, sentence structure and word usage;
4. Arithmetic reasoning and deductive reasoning;
5. Knowledge of basic medical terms; and
6. Other related areas.

HOW TO TAKE A TEST

I. YOU MUST PASS AN EXAMINATION

A. *WHAT EVERY CANDIDATE SHOULD KNOW*

Examination applicants often ask us for help in preparing for the written test. What can I study in advance? What kinds of questions will be asked? How will the test be given? How will the papers be graded?

As an applicant for a civil service examination, you may be wondering about some of these things. Our purpose here is to suggest effective methods of advance study and to describe civil service examinations.

Your chances for success on this examination can be increased if you know how to prepare. Those "pre-examination jitters" can be reduced if you know what to expect. You can even experience an adventure in good citizenship if you know why civil service exams are given.

B. *WHY ARE CIVIL SERVICE EXAMINATIONS GIVEN?*

Civil service examinations are important to you in two ways. As a citizen, you want public jobs filled by employees who know how to do their work. As a job seeker, you want a fair chance to compete for that job on an equal footing with other candidates. The best-known means of accomplishing this two-fold goal is the competitive examination.

Exams are widely publicized throughout the nation. They may be administered for jobs in federal, state, city, municipal, town or village governments or agencies.

Any citizen may apply, with some limitations, such as the age or residence of applicants. Your experience and education may be reviewed to see whether you meet the requirements for the particular examination. When these requirements exist, they are reasonable and applied consistently to all applicants. Thus, a competitive examination may cause you some uneasiness now, but it is your privilege and safeguard.

C. *HOW ARE CIVIL SERVICE EXAMS DEVELOPED?*

Examinations are carefully written by trained technicians who are specialists in the field known as "psychological measurement," in consultation with recognized authorities in the field of work that the test will cover. These experts recommend the subject matter areas or skills to be tested; only those knowledges or skills important to your success on the job are included. The most reliable books and source materials available are used as references. Together, the experts and technicians judge the difficulty level of the questions.

Test technicians know how to phrase questions so that the problem is clearly stated. Their ethics do not permit "trick" or "catch" questions. Questions may have been tried out on sample groups, or subjected to statistical analysis, to determine their usefulness.

Written tests are often used in combination with performance tests, ratings of training and experience, and oral interviews. All of these measures combine to form the best-known means of finding the right person for the right job.

II. HOW TO PASS THE WRITTEN TEST

A. NATURE OF THE EXAMINATION

To prepare intelligently for civil service examinations, you should know how they differ from school examinations you have taken. In school you were assigned certain definite pages to read or subjects to cover. The examination questions were quite detailed and usually emphasized memory. Civil service exams, on the other hand, try to discover your present ability to perform the duties of a position, plus your potentiality to learn these duties. In other words, a civil service exam attempts to predict how successful you will be. Questions cover such a broad area that they cannot be as minute and detailed as school exam questions.

In the public service similar kinds of work, or positions, are grouped together in one "class." This process is known as *position-classification*. All the positions in a class are paid according to the salary range for that class. One class title covers all of these positions, and they are all tested by the same examination.

B. FOUR BASIC STEPS

1) Study the announcement

How, then, can you know what subjects to study? Our best answer is: "Learn as much as possible about the class of positions for which you've applied." The exam will test the knowledge, skills and abilities needed to do the work.

Your most valuable source of information about the position you want is the official exam announcement. This announcement lists the training and experience qualifications. Check these standards and apply only if you come reasonably close to meeting them.

The brief description of the position in the examination announcement offers some clues to the subjects which will be tested. Think about the job itself. Review the duties in your mind. Can you perform them, or are there some in which you are rusty? Fill in the blank spots in your preparation.

Many jurisdictions preview the written test in the exam announcement by including a section called "Knowledge and Abilities Required," "Scope of the Examination," or some similar heading. Here you will find out specifically what fields will be tested.

2) Review your own background

Once you learn in general what the position is all about, and what you need to know to do the work, ask yourself which subjects you already know fairly well and which need improvement. You may wonder whether to concentrate on improving your strong areas or on building some background in your fields of weakness. When the announcement has specified "some knowledge" or "considerable knowledge," or has used adjectives like "beginning principles of..." or "advanced ... methods," you can get a clue as to the number and difficulty of questions to be asked in any given field. More questions, and hence broader coverage, would be included for those subjects which are more important in the work. Now weigh your strengths and weaknesses against the job requirements and prepare accordingly.

3) Determine the level of the position

Another way to tell how intensively you should prepare is to understand the level of the job for which you are applying. Is it the entering level? In other words, is this the position in which beginners in a field of work are hired? Or is it an intermediate or advanced level? Sometimes this is indicated by such words as "Junior" or "Senior" in the class title. Other jurisdictions use Roman numerals to designate the level – Clerk I, Clerk II, for example. The word "Supervisor" sometimes appears in the title. If the level is not indicated by the title, check the description of duties. Will you be working under very close supervision, or will you have responsibility for independent decisions in this work?

4) Choose appropriate study materials

Now that you know the subjects to be examined and the relative amount of each subject to be covered, you can choose suitable study materials. For beginning level jobs, or even advanced ones, if you have a pronounced weakness in some aspect of your training, read a modern, standard textbook in that field. Be sure it is up to date and has general coverage. Such books are normally available at your library, and the librarian will be glad to help you locate one. For entry-level positions, questions of appropriate difficulty are chosen – neither highly advanced questions, nor those too simple. Such questions require careful thought but not advanced training.

If the position for which you are applying is technical or advanced, you will read more advanced, specialized material. If you are already familiar with the basic principles of your field, elementary textbooks would waste your time. Concentrate on advanced textbooks and technical periodicals. Think through the concepts and review difficult problems in your field.

These are all general sources. You can get more ideas on your own initiative, following these leads. For example, training manuals and publications of the government agency which employs workers in your field can be useful, particularly for technical and professional positions. A letter or visit to the government department involved may result in more specific study suggestions, and certainly will provide you with a more definite idea of the exact nature of the position you are seeking.

III. KINDS OF TESTS

Tests are used for purposes other than measuring knowledge and ability to perform specified duties. For some positions, it is equally important to test ability to make adjustments to new situations or to profit from training. In others, basic mental abilities not dependent on information are essential. Questions which test these things may not appear as pertinent to the duties of the position as those which test for knowledge and information. Yet they are often highly important parts of a fair examination. For very general questions, it is almost impossible to help you direct your study efforts. What we can do is to point out some of the more common of these general abilities needed in public service positions and describe some typical questions.

1) General information

Broad, general information has been found useful for predicting job success in some kinds of work. This is tested in a variety of ways, from vocabulary lists to questions about current events. Basic background in some field of work, such as sociology or economics, may be sampled in a group of questions. Often these are principles which have become familiar to most persons through exposure rather than through formal training. It is difficult to advise you how to study for these questions; being alert to the world around you is our best suggestion.

2) Verbal ability

An example of an ability needed in many positions is verbal or language ability. Verbal ability is, in brief, the ability to use and understand words. Vocabulary and grammar tests are typical measures of this ability. Reading comprehension or paragraph interpretation questions are common in many kinds of civil service tests. You are given a paragraph of written material and asked to find its central meaning.

3) Numerical ability

Number skills can be tested by the familiar arithmetic problem, by checking paired lists of numbers to see which are alike and which are different, or by interpreting charts and graphs. In the latter test, a graph may be printed in the test booklet which you are asked to use as the basis for answering questions.

4) Observation

A popular test for law-enforcement positions is the observation test. A picture is shown to you for several minutes, then taken away. Questions about the picture test your ability to observe both details and larger elements.

5) Following directions

In many positions in the public service, the employee must be able to carry out written instructions dependably and accurately. You may be given a chart with several columns, each column listing a variety of information. The questions require you to carry out directions involving the information given in the chart.

6) Skills and aptitudes

Performance tests effectively measure some manual skills and aptitudes. When the skill is one in which you are trained, such as typing or shorthand, you can practice. These tests are often very much like those given in business school or high school courses. For many of the other skills and aptitudes, however, no short-time preparation can be made. Skills and abilities natural to you or that you have developed throughout your lifetime are being tested.

Many of the general questions just described provide all the data needed to answer the questions and ask you to use your reasoning ability to find the answers. Your best preparation for these tests, as well as for tests of facts and ideas, is to be at your physical and mental best. You, no doubt, have your own methods of getting into an exam-taking mood and keeping "in shape." The next section lists some ideas on this subject.

IV. KINDS OF QUESTIONS

Only rarely is the "essay" question, which you answer in narrative form, used in civil service tests. Civil service tests are usually of the short-answer type. Full instructions for answering these questions will be given to you at the examination. But in case this is your first experience with short-answer questions and separate answer sheets, here is what you need to know:

1) Multiple-choice Questions

Most popular of the short-answer questions is the "multiple choice" or "best answer" question. It can be used, for example, to test for factual knowledge, ability to solve problems or judgment in meeting situations found at work.

A multiple-choice question is normally one of three types—

- It can begin with an incomplete statement followed by several possible endings. You are to find the one ending which *best* completes the statement, although some of the others may not be entirely wrong.
- It can also be a complete statement in the form of a question which is answered by choosing one of the statements listed.

- It can be in the form of a problem – again you select the best answer.

Here is an example of a multiple-choice question with a discussion which should give you some clues as to the method for choosing the right answer:

When an employee has a complaint about his assignment, the action which will *best* help him overcome his difficulty is to
- A. discuss his difficulty with his coworkers
- B. take the problem to the head of the organization
- C. take the problem to the person who gave him the assignment
- D. say nothing to anyone about his complaint

In answering this question, you should study each of the choices to find which is best. Consider choice "A" – Certainly an employee may discuss his complaint with fellow employees, but no change or improvement can result, and the complaint remains unresolved. Choice "B" is a poor choice since the head of the organization probably does not know what assignment you have been given, and taking your problem to him is known as "going over the head" of the supervisor. The supervisor, or person who made the assignment, is the person who can clarify it or correct any injustice. Choice "C" is, therefore, correct. To say nothing, as in choice "D," is unwise. Supervisors have and interest in knowing the problems employees are facing, and the employee is seeking a solution to his problem.

2) True/False Questions

The "true/false" or "right/wrong" form of question is sometimes used. Here a complete statement is given. Your job is to decide whether the statement is right or wrong.

SAMPLE: A roaming cell-phone call to a nearby city costs less than a non-roaming call to a distant city.

This statement is wrong, or false, since roaming calls are more expensive.

This is not a complete list of all possible question forms, although most of the others are variations of these common types. You will always get complete directions for answering questions. Be sure you understand *how* to mark your answers – ask questions until you do.

V. RECORDING YOUR ANSWERS

Computer terminals are used more and more today for many different kinds of exams.
For an examination with very few applicants, you may be told to record your answers in the test booklet itself. Separate answer sheets are much more common. If this separate answer sheet is to be scored by machine – and this is often the case – it is highly important that you mark your answers correctly in order to get credit.
An electronic scoring machine is often used in civil service offices because of the speed with which papers can be scored. Machine-scored answer sheets must be marked with a pencil, which will be given to you. This pencil has a high graphite content which responds to the electronic scoring machine. As a matter of fact, stray dots may register as answers, so do not let your pencil rest on the answer sheet while you are pondering the correct answer. Also, if your pencil lead breaks or is otherwise defective, ask for another.

Since the answer sheet will be dropped in a slot in the scoring machine, be careful not to bend the corners or get the paper crumpled.

The answer sheet normally has five vertical columns of numbers, with 30 numbers to a column. These numbers correspond to the question numbers in your test booklet. After each number, going across the page are four or five pairs of dotted lines. These short dotted lines have small letters or numbers above them. The first two pairs may also have a "T" or "F" above the letters. This indicates that the first two pairs only are to be used if the questions are of the true-false type. If the questions are multiple choice, disregard the "T" and "F" and pay attention only to the small letters or numbers.

Answer your questions in the manner of the sample that follows:

32. The largest city in the United States is
    A. Washington, D.C.
    B. New York City
    C. Chicago
    D. Detroit
    E. San Francisco

1) Choose the answer you think is best. (New York City is the largest, so "B" is correct.)
2) Find the row of dotted lines numbered the same as the question you are answering. (Find row number 32)
3) Find the pair of dotted lines corresponding to the answer. (Find the pair of lines under the mark "B.")
4) Make a solid black mark between the dotted lines.

VI. BEFORE THE TEST

Common sense will help you find procedures to follow to get ready for an examination. Too many of us, however, overlook these sensible measures. Indeed, nervousness and fatigue have been found to be the most serious reasons why applicants fail to do their best on civil service tests. Here is a list of reminders:

- Begin your preparation early – Don't wait until the last minute to go scurrying around for books and materials or to find out what the position is all about.
- Prepare continuously – An hour a night for a week is better than an all-night cram session. This has been definitely established. What is more, a night a week for a month will return better dividends than crowding your study into a shorter period of time.
- Locate the place of the exam – You have been sent a notice telling you when and where to report for the examination. If the location is in a different town or otherwise unfamiliar to you, it would be well to inquire the best route and learn something about the building.
- Relax the night before the test – Allow your mind to rest. Do not study at all that night. Plan some mild recreation or diversion; then go to bed early and get a good night's sleep.
- Get up early enough to make a leisurely trip to the place for the test – This way unforeseen events, traffic snarls, unfamiliar buildings, etc. will not upset you.
- Dress comfortably – A written test is not a fashion show. You will be known by number and not by name, so wear something comfortable.

- Leave excess paraphernalia at home – Shopping bags and odd bundles will get in your way. You need bring only the items mentioned in the official notice you received; usually everything you need is provided. Do not bring reference books to the exam. They will only confuse those last minutes and be taken away from you when in the test room.
- Arrive somewhat ahead of time – If because of transportation schedules you must get there very early, bring a newspaper or magazine to take your mind off yourself while waiting.
- Locate the examination room – When you have found the proper room, you will be directed to the seat or part of the room where you will sit. Sometimes you are given a sheet of instructions to read while you are waiting. Do not fill out any forms until you are told to do so; just read them and be prepared.
- Relax and prepare to listen to the instructions
- If you have any physical problem that may keep you from doing your best, be sure to tell the test administrator. If you are sick or in poor health, you really cannot do your best on the exam. You can come back and take the test some other time.

VII. AT THE TEST

The day of the test is here and you have the test booklet in your hand. The temptation to get going is very strong. Caution! There is more to success than knowing the right answers. You must know how to identify your papers and understand variations in the type of short-answer question used in this particular examination. Follow these suggestions for maximum results from your efforts:

1) Cooperate with the monitor

The test administrator has a duty to create a situation in which you can be as much at ease as possible. He will give instructions, tell you when to begin, check to see that you are marking your answer sheet correctly, and so on. He is not there to guard you, although he will see that your competitors do not take unfair advantage. He wants to help you do your best.

2) Listen to all instructions

Don't jump the gun! Wait until you understand all directions. In most civil service tests you get more time than you need to answer the questions. So don't be in a hurry. Read each word of instructions until you clearly understand the meaning. Study the examples, listen to all announcements and follow directions. Ask questions if you do not understand what to do.

3) Identify your papers

Civil service exams are usually identified by number only. You will be assigned a number; you must not put your name on your test papers. Be sure to copy your number correctly. Since more than one exam may be given, copy your exact examination title.

4) Plan your time

Unless you are told that a test is a "speed" or "rate of work" test, speed itself is usually not important. Time enough to answer all the questions will be provided, but this does not mean that you have all day. An overall time limit has been set. Divide the total time (in minutes) by the number of questions to determine the approximate time you have for each question.

5) Do not linger over difficult questions

If you come across a difficult question, mark it with a paper clip (useful to have along) and come back to it when you have been through the booklet. One caution if you do this – be sure to skip a number on your answer sheet as well. Check often to be sure that you have not lost your place and that you are marking in the row numbered the same as the question you are answering.

6) Read the questions

Be sure you know what the question asks! Many capable people are unsuccessful because they failed to *read* the questions correctly.

7) Answer all questions

Unless you have been instructed that a penalty will be deducted for incorrect answers, it is better to guess than to omit a question.

8) Speed tests

It is often better NOT to guess on speed tests. It has been found that on timed tests people are tempted to spend the last few seconds before time is called in marking answers at random – without even reading them – in the hope of picking up a few extra points. To discourage this practice, the instructions may warn you that your score will be "corrected" for guessing. That is, a penalty will be applied. The incorrect answers will be deducted from the correct ones, or some other penalty formula will be used.

9) Review your answers

If you finish before time is called, go back to the questions you guessed or omitted to give them further thought. Review other answers if you have time.

10) Return your test materials

If you are ready to leave before others have finished or time is called, take ALL your materials to the monitor and leave quietly. Never take any test material with you. The monitor can discover whose papers are not complete, and taking a test booklet may be grounds for disqualification.

VIII. EXAMINATION TECHNIQUES

1) Read the general instructions carefully. These are usually printed on the first page of the exam booklet. As a rule, these instructions refer to the timing of the examination; the fact that you should not start work until the signal and must stop work at a signal, etc. If there are any *special* instructions, such as a choice of questions to be answered, make sure that you note this instruction carefully.

2) When you are ready to start work on the examination, that is as soon as the signal has been given, read the instructions to each question booklet, underline any key words or phrases, such as *least, best, outline, describe* and the like. In this way you will tend to answer as requested rather than discover on reviewing your paper that you *listed without describing*, that you selected the *worst* choice rather than the *best* choice, etc.

3) If the examination is of the objective or multiple-choice type – that is, each question will also give a series of possible answers: A, B, C or D, and you are called upon to select the best answer and write the letter next to that answer on your answer paper – it is advisable to start answering each question in turn. There may be anywhere from 50 to 100 such questions in the three or four hours allotted and you can see how much time would be taken if you read through all the questions before beginning to answer any. Furthermore, if you come across a question or group of questions which you know would be difficult to answer, it would undoubtedly affect your handling of all the other questions.

4) If the examination is of the essay type and contains but a few questions, it is a moot point as to whether you should read all the questions before starting to answer any one. Of course, if you are given a choice – say five out of seven and the like – then it is essential to read all the questions so you can eliminate the two that are most difficult. If, however, you are asked to answer all the questions, there may be danger in trying to answer the easiest one first because you may find that you will spend too much time on it. The best technique is to answer the first question, then proceed to the second, etc.

5) Time your answers. Before the exam begins, write down the time it started, then add the time allowed for the examination and write down the time it must be completed, then divide the time available somewhat as follows:
    - If 3-1/2 hours are allowed, that would be 210 minutes. If you have 80 objective-type questions, that would be an average of 2-1/2 minutes per question. Allow yourself no more than 2 minutes per question, or a total of 160 minutes, which will permit about 50 minutes to review.
    - If for the time allotment of 210 minutes there are 7 essay questions to answer, that would average about 30 minutes a question. Give yourself only 25 minutes per question so that you have about 35 minutes to review.

6) The most important instruction is to *read each question* and make sure you know what is wanted. The second most important instruction is to *time yourself properly* so that you answer every question. The third most important instruction is to *answer every question*. Guess if you have to but include something for each question. Remember that you will receive no credit for a blank and will probably receive some credit if you write something in answer to an essay question. If you guess a letter – say "B" for a multiple-choice question – you may have guessed right. If you leave a blank as an answer to a multiple-choice question, the examiners may respect your feelings but it will not add a point to your score. Some exams may penalize you for wrong answers, so in such cases *only*, you may not want to guess unless you have some basis for your answer.

7) Suggestions
    a. Objective-type questions
        1. Examine the question booklet for proper sequence of pages and questions
        2. Read all instructions carefully
        3. Skip any question which seems too difficult; return to it after all other questions have been answered
        4. Apportion your time properly; do not spend too much time on any single question or group of questions

5. Note and underline key words – *all, most, fewest, least, best, worst, same, opposite*, etc.
6. Pay particular attention to negatives
7. Note unusual option, e.g., unduly long, short, complex, different or similar in content to the body of the question
8. Observe the use of "hedging" words – *probably, may, most likely*, etc.
9. Make sure that your answer is put next to the same number as the question
10. Do not second-guess unless you have good reason to believe the second answer is definitely more correct
11. Cross out original answer if you decide another answer is more accurate; do not erase until you are ready to hand your paper in
12. Answer all questions; guess unless instructed otherwise
13. Leave time for review

   b. Essay questions
1. Read each question carefully
2. Determine exactly what is wanted. Underline key words or phrases.
3. Decide on outline or paragraph answer
4. Include many different points and elements unless asked to develop any one or two points or elements
5. Show impartiality by giving pros and cons unless directed to select one side only
6. Make and write down any assumptions you find necessary to answer the questions
7. Watch your English, grammar, punctuation and choice of words
8. Time your answers; don't crowd material

8) Answering the essay question

Most essay questions can be answered by framing the specific response around several key words or ideas. Here are a few such key words or ideas:

M's: manpower, materials, methods, money, management
P's: purpose, program, policy, plan, procedure, practice, problems, pitfalls, personnel, public relations

   a. Six basic steps in handling problems:
1. Preliminary plan and background development
2. Collect information, data and facts
3. Analyze and interpret information, data and facts
4. Analyze and develop solutions as well as make recommendations
5. Prepare report and sell recommendations
6. Install recommendations and follow up effectiveness

   b. Pitfalls to avoid
1. *Taking things for granted* – A statement of the situation does not necessarily imply that each of the elements is necessarily true; for example, a complaint may be invalid and biased so that all that can be taken for granted is that a complaint has been registered

2. *Considering only one side of a situation* – Wherever possible, indicate several alternatives and then point out the reasons you selected the best one
3. *Failing to indicate follow up* – Whenever your answer indicates action on your part, make certain that you will take proper follow-up action to see how successful your recommendations, procedures or actions turn out to be
4. *Taking too long in answering any single question* – Remember to time your answers properly

IX. AFTER THE TEST

Scoring procedures differ in detail among civil service jurisdictions although the general principles are the same. Whether the papers are hand-scored or graded by machine we have described, they are nearly always graded by number. That is, the person who marks the paper knows only the number – never the name – of the applicant. Not until all the papers have been graded will they be matched with names. If other tests, such as training and experience or oral interview ratings have been given, scores will be combined. Different parts of the examination usually have different weights. For example, the written test might count 60 percent of the final grade, and a rating of training and experience 40 percent. In many jurisdictions, veterans will have a certain number of points added to their grades.

After the final grade has been determined, the names are placed in grade order and an eligible list is established. There are various methods for resolving ties between those who get the same final grade – probably the most common is to place first the name of the person whose application was received first. Job offers are made from the eligible list in the order the names appear on it. You will be notified of your grade and your rank as soon as all these computations have been made. This will be done as rapidly as possible.

People who are found to meet the requirements in the announcement are called "eligibles." Their names are put on a list of eligible candidates. An eligible's chances of getting a job depend on how high he stands on this list and how fast agencies are filling jobs from the list.

When a job is to be filled from a list of eligibles, the agency asks for the names of people on the list of eligibles for that job. When the civil service commission receives this request, it sends to the agency the names of the three people highest on this list. Or, if the job to be filled has specialized requirements, the office sends the agency the names of the top three persons who meet these requirements from the general list.

The appointing officer makes a choice from among the three people whose names were sent to him. If the selected person accepts the appointment, the names of the others are put back on the list to be considered for future openings.

That is the rule in hiring from all kinds of eligible lists, whether they are for typist, carpenter, chemist, or something else. For every vacancy, the appointing officer has his choice of any one of the top three eligibles on the list. This explains why the person whose name is on top of the list sometimes does not get an appointment when some of the persons lower on the list do. If the appointing officer chooses the second or third eligible, the No. 1 eligible does not get a job at once, but stays on the list until he is appointed or the list is terminated.

X. HOW TO PASS THE INTERVIEW TEST

The examination for which you applied requires an oral interview test. You have already taken the written test and you are now being called for the interview test – the final part of the formal examination.

You may think that it is not possible to prepare for an interview test and that there are no procedures to follow during an interview. Our purpose is to point out some things you can do in advance that will help you and some good rules to follow and pitfalls to avoid while you are being interviewed.

What is an interview supposed to test?

The written examination is designed to test the technical knowledge and competence of the candidate; the oral is designed to evaluate intangible qualities, not readily measured otherwise, and to establish a list showing the relative fitness of each candidate – as measured against his competitors – for the position sought. Scoring is not on the basis of "right" and "wrong," but on a sliding scale of values ranging from "not passable" to "outstanding." As a matter of fact, it is possible to achieve a relatively low score without a single "incorrect" answer because of evident weakness in the qualities being measured.

Occasionally, an examination may consist entirely of an oral test – either an individual or a group oral. In such cases, information is sought concerning the technical knowledges and abilities of the candidate, since there has been no written examination for this purpose. More commonly, however, an oral test is used to supplement a written examination.

Who conducts interviews?

The composition of oral boards varies among different jurisdictions. In nearly all, a representative of the personnel department serves as chairman. One of the members of the board may be a representative of the department in which the candidate would work. In some cases, "outside experts" are used, and, frequently, a businessman or some other representative of the general public is asked to serve. Labor and management or other special groups may be represented. The aim is to secure the services of experts in the appropriate field.

However the board is composed, it is a good idea (and not at all improper or unethical) to ascertain in advance of the interview who the members are and what groups they represent. When you are introduced to them, you will have some idea of their backgrounds and interests, and at least you will not stutter and stammer over their names.

What should be done before the interview?

While knowledge about the board members is useful and takes some of the surprise element out of the interview, there is other preparation which is more substantive. It *is* possible to prepare for an oral interview – in several ways:

1) Keep a copy of your application and review it carefully before the interview

This may be the only document before the oral board, and the starting point of the interview. Know what education and experience you have listed there, and the sequence and dates of all of it. Sometimes the board will ask you to review the highlights of your experience for them; you should not have to hem and haw doing it.

2) Study the class specification and the examination announcement

Usually, the oral board has one or both of these to guide them. The qualities, characteristics or knowledges required by the position sought are stated in these documents. They offer valuable clues as to the nature of the oral interview. For example, if the job involves supervisory responsibilities, the announcement will usually indicate that knowledge of modern supervisory methods and the qualifications of the candidate as a supervisor will be tested. If so, you can expect such questions, frequently in the form of a hypothetical situation which you are expected to solve. NEVER go into an oral without knowledge of the duties and responsibilities of the job you seek.

3) Think through each qualification required

Try to visualize the kind of questions you would ask if you were a board member. How well could you answer them? Try especially to appraise your own knowledge and background in each area, *measured against the job sought*, and identify any areas in which you are weak. Be critical and realistic – do not flatter yourself.

4) Do some general reading in areas in which you feel you may be weak

For example, if the job involves supervision and your past experience has NOT, some general reading in supervisory methods and practices, particularly in the field of human relations, might be useful. Do NOT study agency procedures or detailed manuals. The oral board will be testing your understanding and capacity, not your memory.

5) Get a good night's sleep and watch your general health and mental attitude

You will want a clear head at the interview. Take care of a cold or any other minor ailment, and of course, no hangovers.

What should be done on the day of the interview?

Now comes the day of the interview itself. Give yourself plenty of time to get there. Plan to arrive somewhat ahead of the scheduled time, particularly if your appointment is in the fore part of the day. If a previous candidate fails to appear, the board might be ready for you a bit early. By early afternoon an oral board is almost invariably behind schedule if there are many candidates, and you may have to wait. Take along a book or magazine to read, or your application to review, but leave any extraneous material in the waiting room when you go in for your interview. In any event, relax and compose yourself.

The matter of dress is important. The board is forming impressions about you – from your experience, your manners, your attitude, and your appearance. Give your personal appearance careful attention. Dress your best, but not your flashiest. Choose conservative, appropriate clothing, and be sure it is immaculate. This is a business interview, and your appearance should indicate that you regard it as such. Besides, being well groomed and properly dressed will help boost your confidence.

Sooner or later, someone will call your name and escort you into the interview room. *This is it.* From here on you are on your own. It is too late for any more preparation. But remember, you asked for this opportunity to prove your fitness, and you are here because your request was granted.

What happens when you go in?

The usual sequence of events will be as follows: The clerk (who is often the board stenographer) will introduce you to the chairman of the oral board, who will introduce you to the other members of the board. Acknowledge the introductions before you sit down. Do not be surprised if you find a microphone facing you or a stenotypist sitting by. Oral interviews are usually recorded in the event of an appeal or other review.

Usually the chairman of the board will open the interview by reviewing the highlights of your education and work experience from your application – primarily for the benefit of the other members of the board, as well as to get the material into the record. Do not interrupt or comment unless there is an error or significant misinterpretation; if that is the case, do not hesitate. But do not quibble about insignificant matters. Also, he will usually ask you some question about your education, experience or your present job – partly to get you to start talking and to establish the interviewing "rapport." He may start the actual questioning, or turn it over to one of the other members. Frequently, each member undertakes the questioning on a particular area, one in which he is perhaps most competent, so you can expect each member to participate in the examination. Because time is limited, you may also expect some rather abrupt switches in the direction the questioning takes, so do not be upset by it. Normally, a board member will not pursue a single line of questioning unless he discovers a particular strength or weakness.

After each member has participated, the chairman will usually ask whether any member has any further questions, then will ask you if you have anything you wish to add. Unless you are expecting this question, it may floor you. Worse, it may start you off on an extended, extemporaneous speech. The board is not usually seeking more information. The question is principally to offer you a last opportunity to present further qualifications or to indicate that you have nothing to add. So, if you feel that a significant qualification or characteristic has been overlooked, it is proper to point it out in a sentence or so. Do not compliment the board on the thoroughness of their examination – they have been sketchy, and you know it. If you wish, merely say, "No thank you, I have nothing further to add." This is a point where you can "talk yourself out" of a good impression or fail to present an important bit of information. Remember, *you close the interview yourself*.

The chairman will then say, "That is all, Mr. _____, thank you." Do not be startled; the interview is over, and quicker than you think. Thank him, gather your belongings and take your leave. Save your sigh of relief for the other side of the door.

How to put your best foot forward

Throughout this entire process, you may feel that the board individually and collectively is trying to pierce your defenses, seek out your hidden weaknesses and embarrass and confuse you. Actually, this is not true. They are obliged to make an appraisal of your qualifications for the job you are seeking, and they want to see you in your best light. Remember, they must interview all candidates and a non-cooperative candidate may become a failure in spite of their best efforts to bring out his qualifications. Here are 15 suggestions that will help you:

1) Be natural – Keep your attitude confident, not cocky

If you are not confident that you can do the job, do not expect the board to be. Do not apologize for your weaknesses, try to bring out your strong points. The board is interested in a positive, not negative, presentation. Cockiness will antagonize any board member and make him wonder if you are covering up a weakness by a false show of strength.

2) Get comfortable, but don't lounge or sprawl

Sit erectly but not stiffly. A careless posture may lead the board to conclude that you are careless in other things, or at least that you are not impressed by the importance of the occasion. Either conclusion is natural, even if incorrect. Do not fuss with your clothing, a pencil or an ashtray. Your hands may occasionally be useful to emphasize a point; do not let them become a point of distraction.

3) Do not wisecrack or make small talk

This is a serious situation, and your attitude should show that you consider it as such. Further, the time of the board is limited – they do not want to waste it, and neither should you.

4) Do not exaggerate your experience or abilities

In the first place, from information in the application or other interviews and sources, the board may know more about you than you think. Secondly, you probably will not get away with it. An experienced board is rather adept at spotting such a situation, so do not take the chance.

5) If you know a board member, do not make a point of it, yet do not hide it

Certainly you are not fooling him, and probably not the other members of the board. Do not try to take advantage of your acquaintanceship – it will probably do you little good.

6) Do not dominate the interview

Let the board do that. They will give you the clues – do not assume that you have to do all the talking. Realize that the board has a number of questions to ask you, and do not try to take up all the interview time by showing off your extensive knowledge of the answer to the first one.

7) Be attentive

You only have 20 minutes or so, and you should keep your attention at its sharpest throughout. When a member is addressing a problem or question to you, give him your undivided attention. Address your reply principally to him, but do not exclude the other board members.

8) Do not interrupt

A board member may be stating a problem for you to analyze. He will ask you a question when the time comes. Let him state the problem, and wait for the question.

9) Make sure you understand the question

Do not try to answer until you are sure what the question is. If it is not clear, restate it in your own words or ask the board member to clarify it for you. However, do not haggle about minor elements.

10) Reply promptly but not hastily

A common entry on oral board rating sheets is "candidate responded readily," or "candidate hesitated in replies." Respond as promptly and quickly as you can, but do not jump to a hasty, ill-considered answer.

11) Do not be peremptory in your answers

A brief answer is proper – but do not fire your answer back. That is a losing game from your point of view. The board member can probably ask questions much faster than you can answer them.

12) Do not try to create the answer you think the board member wants

He is interested in what kind of mind you have and how it works – not in playing games. Furthermore, he can usually spot this practice and will actually grade you down on it.

13) Do not switch sides in your reply merely to agree with a board member

Frequently, a member will take a contrary position merely to draw you out and to see if you are willing and able to defend your point of view. Do not start a debate, yet do not surrender a good position. If a position is worth taking, it is worth defending.

14) Do not be afraid to admit an error in judgment if you are shown to be wrong

The board knows that you are forced to reply without any opportunity for careful consideration. Your answer may be demonstrably wrong. If so, admit it and get on with the interview.

15) Do not dwell at length on your present job

The opening question may relate to your present assignment. Answer the question but do not go into an extended discussion. You are being examined for a *new* job, not your present one. As a matter of fact, try to phrase ALL your answers in terms of the job for which you are being examined.

Basis of Rating

Probably you will forget most of these "do's" and "don'ts" when you walk into the oral interview room. Even remembering them all will not ensure you a passing grade. Perhaps you did not have the qualifications in the first place. But remembering them will help you to put your best foot forward, without treading on the toes of the board members.

Rumor and popular opinion to the contrary notwithstanding, an oral board wants you to make the best appearance possible. They know you are under pressure – but they also want to see how you respond to it as a guide to what your reaction would be under the pressures of the job you seek. They will be influenced by the degree of poise you display, the personal traits you show and the manner in which you respond.

ABOUT THIS BOOK

This book contains tests divided into Examination Sections. Go through each test, answering every question in the margin. We have also attached a sample answer sheet at the back of the book that can be removed and used. At the end of each test look at the answer key and check your answers. On the ones you got wrong, look at the right answer choice and learn. Do not fill in the answers first. Do not memorize the questions and answers, but understand the answer and principles involved. On your test, the questions will likely be different from the samples. Questions are changed and new ones added. If you understand these past questions you should have success with any changes that arise. Tests may consist of several types of questions. We have additional books on each subject should more study be advisable or necessary for you. Finally, the more you study, the better prepared you will be. This book is intended to be the last thing you study before you walk into the examination room. Prior study of relevant texts is also recommended. NLC publishes some of these in our Fundamental Series. Knowledge and good sense are important factors in passing your exam. Good luck also helps. So now study this Passbook, absorb the material contained within and take that knowledge into the examination. Then do your best to pass that exam.

EXAMINATION SECTION

EDUCATING AND INTERACTING WITH THE PUBLIC

These questions test for knowledge of techniques used to interact effectively with individual citizens and/or community groups, to educate or inform them about topics of concern, to publicize or clarify agency programs or policies, to negotiate conflicts or resolve complaints, and to represent one's agency or program in a manner in keeping with good public relations practices. Questions may also cover interacting with others in cooperative efforts of public outreach or service. There will be 15 questions in this subject area on the written test.

TEST TASK:
You will be presented with a variety of situations in which you must apply knowledge of how best to interact with other people.

SAMPLE QUESTION:
A person approaches you expressing anger about a recent action by your department. Which one of the following should be your first response to this person?

A. Interrupt to say you cannot discuss the situation until he calms down.
B. Say you are sorry that he has been negatively affected by your department's action.
C. Listen and express understanding that he has been upset by your department's action.
D. Give him an explanation of the reasons for your department's action.

The correct answer to this sample question is choice C

C. SOLUTION:

Choice A *is not correct.* It would be inappropriate to interrupt. In addition, saying that you cannot discuss the situation until the person calms down will likely aggravate him further.

Choice B *is not correct.* Apologizing for your department's action implies that the action was improper.

Choice C *is the correct answer to this question.* By listening and expressing understanding that your department's action has upset him, you demonstrate that you have heard and understand his feelings and point of view.

Choice D *is not correct.* While an explanation of the reasons for the action may be appropriate at a later time, at this moment the person is angry and would not be receptive to such an explanation.

EXAMINATION SECTION
TEST 1

DIRECTIONS: Each question or incomplete statement is followed by several suggested answers or completions. Select the one that BEST answers the question or completes the statement. *PRINT THE LETTER OF THE CORRECT ANSWER IN THE SPACE AT THE RIGHT.*

1. Which of the following is a behavior that can impact customer service? 1.____
   A. Greeting customers promptly
   B. Believing in a positive mission statement
   C. Giving great service
   D. Poor work attitude

2. What are vital behaviors? 2.____
   A. Ones that are mandated by law
   B. Specific actions that have the maximum impact on customer service
   C. Of no particular importance when influencing employees
   D. The same as good attitudes

3. Of the following, the MOST effective icebreaker when greeting a local citizen in your office would be: 3.____
   A. Talking about local interests such as a sports team or the weather
   B. Expression appreciation for the citizen visiting you today
   C. Finding out and expressing interest in something the citizen shows interest in
   D. All of the above

4. Which of the following actions would get citizens to interact with you and, therefore, the government you represent? 4.____
   A. Inviting the citizens to fill out a survey on government services
   B. Helping the citizen find answers to questions about your department
   C. Both A and B
   D. None of the above

5. Of the following options, the BIGGEST issue with not greeting a citizen promptly is: 5.____
   A. He or she might not leave as quickly as you'd like them to
   B. The department misses an opportunity to establish a positive relationship
   C. They may estimate that their wait was shorter than it actually was
   D. Both A and C

6. Which of the following actions is important to take when someone makes an oral presentation to a large group of local residents? 6.____
   A. Relax the audience by moving back and forth when speaking
   B. Avoid eye contact with anyone in the audience
   C. Speak loudly enough for all to hear your message
   D. Turn your back to the audience when presenting visual aids

7. Of the following techniques for writing effective communication (i.e., letters about local tax bills) to residents, which of the following helps a person consistently stay on message the MOST?
   A. Preparing outlines
   B. Development and inclusion of charts
   C. Consulting references
   D. Asking questions

8. Persuasive messages that ask a person to do something should be communicated in a way that makes it easy for that person to
   A. plan accordingly
   B. answer politely
   C. organize logically
   D. respond positively

9. If a city department wishes to emphasize customer service skills such as courtesy and friendliness, when should said department focus on these skills?
   A. When designing their facilities
   B. During market research
   C. When meeting for technology planning
   D. During the hiring process

10. If a department realizes it needs to improve its technology to better meet resident demands and desires, this would have to result from a business activity known as
    A. continuity improvement
    B. business process management
    C. employee training and in-service
    D. organizational positioning

11. When in the distribution channel business, what is an important thing to keep in mind concerning customers?
    A. Most expect low service levels
    B. Many want immediate delivery
    C. Everyone defines service differently
    D. A number of customers tend to refuse late shipments

12. When persuading a citizen to go along with a proposed change from their initial query, you should
    A. explain how the change will benefit them
    B. tell them you have a better way of doing things
    C. minimize the amount of information you share with them
    D. reinforce your ideas with facts and statistics

13. Which of the following statements is TRUE regarding use of the internet to administer questionnaires?
    A. Interviewers are more likely to influence respondents' answers online
    B. Online questionnaires require more time for data entry and collection
    C. Respondents are more likely to misunderstand online questionnaires
    D. Data entry and administrative costs are higher for online questionnaires

14. After a series of notable scandals, a government organization wants the public to perceive it as more trustworthy and embarks on an advertising campaign to aid the makeover. What goal does this illustrate?
    A. Projecting a certain image
    B. Achieving stability
    C. Increasing customer service and productivity
    D. All of the above

14.____

15. When presenting information to a small group of town residents, you decide to use presentation software to prepare your multimedia presentation.
    What is the purpose of using this software?
    A. To develop websites
    B. To maintain customer files
    C. To access online resources
    D. To support your report findings

15.____

16. A current trend in interaction with citizens in order to build loyal customer relationships and enhance service levels focuses on optimizing the use of
    A. independent agents
    B. internet web sites
    C. satellite roving devices
    D. service rating advisors

16.____

17. Which of the following would be an excellent example of a parks department official empathizing with a citizen's objection?
    A. "I understand how you feel."
    B. "You must think the price is too high."
    C. "Everyone knows this is how this process works."
    D. "I really don't see what you don't understand about this."

17.____

18. Customer service experts who use the services and products they are in charge of dispensing are able to suggest appropriate substitute services and products because of their own personal
    A. preference
    B. feelings
    C. experience
    D. opinion

18.____

19. An official should always attempt to answer a citizen's questions thoroughly and explain the benefits of their services so that the citizen will
    A. make a quicker decision
    B. be in a state of indecision
    C. think about making a decision
    D. feel better about the decision

19.____

20. One should be able to adjust his customer-service style from one citizen to another so that he can appeal to each citizen's
    A. natural aptitude
    B. unique personality
    C. hidden objection
    D. internal ability

20.____

21. In order to attract local residents and encourage them to make use of a new recreation facility, what should a parks department director do?
    A. Market the site's benefits
    B. Host trade shows
    C. Distribute press kits
    D. Host special community events

21.____

22. What kind of question is a person asking if they ask the following: "What level of service would you like today?"
    A. Interpretive
    B. Impersonal
    C. Open-ended
    D. Assumptive

22.____

23. Your department holds a meeting to identify community issues with which they can involve themselves.
    Which of the following options should the department consider when deciding which community issue to involve themselves with?
    It should
    A. contribute to the social good
    B. earn a reasonable profit
    C. boost loyalty among citizens
    D. support controversial topics

23.____

24. If a person's thoughts, emotions and physical sensations interfere with their listening skills, that is referred to as
    A. cultural diversity
    B. internal noise
    C. cultural norms
    D. external noise

24.____

25. Which of the following is NOT a characteristic of information literacy?
    The ability to
    A. use information to manipulate others
    B. determine what information is needed for a presentation
    C. find information relevant to a topic
    D. use information to create new knowledge

25.____

KEY (CORRECT ANSWERS)

1. A
2. B
3. D
4. C
5. B

6. C
7. A
8. D
9. D
10. B

11. C
12. A
13. C
14. A
15. D

16. B
17. A
18. C
19. D
20. B

21. D
22. C
23. A
24. B
25. A

TEST 2

DIRECTIONS: Each question or incomplete statement is followed by several suggested answers or completions. Select the one that BEST answers the question or completes the statement. *PRINT THE LETTER OF THE CORRECT ANSWER IN THE SPACE AT THE RIGHT.*

1. When preparing to deliver a speech, what is the purpose of writing key points on notecards and then placing those cards in order of their importance?
   A. To verify their authenticity
   B. To access files
   C. To revise facts
   D. To organize information

   1.____

2. A city official who is originally from Ecuador meets with a citizen who has moved to the area from London, England. When the official attempts to shake the citizen's hand, he backs away.
   What cultural issue should the official be aware of next time to avoid this misstep?
   A. Punctuality
   B. Personal space preferences
   C. Appearance
   D. Language variances

   2.____

3. Someone who demonstrates self-confidence has which of the following characteristics?
   A. They take few risks because they fear making mistakes
   B. They exhibit aggressive behavior when expressing their opinion
   C. They realize that mistakes are a part of personal growth
   D. They are overly concerned with what others say about them

   3.____

4. A town clerk is talking with a resident about fees associated with filing a building permit when the resident interrupts and says, "I refuse to pay for this. These fees are preposterous!"
   If the clerk wishes to reply in the most professional manner possible, they should do which of the following?
   A. Attempt to explain the benefits of the service
   B. Stop helping the resident and find someone else to help
   C. Ask a supervisor to help convince the resident of the service's merits
   D. Thank the resident politely for coming in

   4.____

5. You are working with a village resident who asks you questions about aspects of zoning ordinances that you are clearly not familiar with. A coworker overhears the conversation and offers to help.
   What is the FIRST thing you should do?
   A. Politely refuse the help and attempt to answer the resident's questions anyway
   B. Accept the offer of help and listen to the answers the coworker gives to the resident
   C. Ignore the coworker; they only want to look good in front of your supervisor
   D. Let the other associate take over and look for a new resident to help

   5.____

6. A resident comes up to an employee in the public works department holding his village-issued recycling container. He says he received the pail a month ago and it already has a cracked handle. As a result his lawn is constantly littered with plastic bottles.
   What is the FIRST thing the employee should say?
   A. "There's no reason it should be cracked. We should have another; I will check for you."
   B. "We've never had anyone make this complaint before. What did you or your child do to it?"
   C. "Are you sure you the village provided this pail? Do you have a receipt?"
   D. "We've had a lot of issues with that item. You should probably contact the manufacturer."

7. When a person first encounters an employee and forms a lasting mental image of that employee and, therefore, the organization, that is called
   A. attitude impact   B. self-confidence
   C. first impression   D. workplace ethics

8. Which of the following convey to citizens that their representative is professional?
   A. No wrinkles, creases or stains   B. No large, loud prints
   C. Well-tailored, formal clothing   D. All of the above

9. A town clerk is put in charge of email communications for the department and asks you for help.
   Which of the following would NOT be considered good email etiquette?
   A. Keeping emails brief and to the point
   B. Putting the purpose of the email in the subject field
   C. Sending humorous YouTube videos and personal emails to customers
   D. Using a signature that includes contact information that follows your message

10. A building department director is holding a meeting for individual building managers and is just about to conclude when another manager shows up late.
    Which of the following actions would be the BEST to take?
    A. Thank the manager for stopping by and pause the meeting momentarily to fill him or her in on what they missed.
    B. Once the meeting is over, remind the manager that punctuality is incredibly important to your department. Then once they seem to understand the importance of being on time, fill them in on what they missed.
    C. Openly criticize the manager in front of everyone else for being tardy. Once you've criticized them, fill them in on what they missed.
    D. Slightly nod to the manager when they enter, but continue the meeting without bringing them up to speed. Once the meeting concludes, fill the manager in if the wish to be brought up to speed.

11. You are running 15 minutes late to a meeting with a constituent. 11.____
    What should you do?
    A. Call the constituent and tell them you will be there in a few minutes.
    B. The constituent won't mind waiting. Fifteen minutes is not that long of a wait.
    C. Have your coworker talk to the constituent and tell them you were involved in a minor traffic accident that is causing you to be delayed.
    D. Pretend like you thought the meeting was supposed to be on a different day. Send an email apologizing for the inconvenience.

12. A longtime friend has stopped at your work to visit you before they fly home. 12.____
    You are currently meeting with the local civic association when he shows up.
    What should you do?
    A. Have your friend join the meeting and introduce him to the group.
    B. Tell your friend to wait in the break room/cafeteria and meet him when you finish up your meeting.
    C. Stop the meeting immediately and tell the group to reschedule with you tomorrow. You also let them know they will have priority in terms of meeting times.
    D. Speed through the rest of the meeting and do not stop to ask if anyone has any questions. Then find your friend afterwards.

13. A fellow clerk is filling out forms with a local resident when you notice your favorite 13.____
    song starts playing from your computer. You
    A. dance around the office after blasting the music on your speakers
    B. listen to the music with your headphones at a loud volume so that the clerk and resident can hear a muted version of the song
    C. listen to the music with your headphones in at a low volume so that you do not disturb others and are still accessible in case you are needed
    D. listen to your music with noise-cancelling headphones, so that you cannot hear others if they request your attention

14. As recreation director, you have an important meeting with members of a local 14.____
    youth sports organization and all agree to meet around dinner time.
    Where should you bring them for the dinner meeting?
    A. Ask them their preference for food and pick the corresponding restaurant
    B. An upscale French restaurant known for its romantic ambience
    C. A sports bar that will be airing an important playoff game
    D. Order Chinese food and invite them to the office

15. A city employee has an important presentation in front of a community group today, but 15.____
    it is also "Casual Friday."
    How should the employee dress? Why?
    A. Dress casually. The residents will understand that Casual Fridays are for casual dress, so they will not be upset.
    B. Business casual. A city employee wants to assure the community that they handle business the way they dress, which means a smart, but comfortable look.

C. A little nicer than normally, but nothing too formal. This way they are still comfortable, but the residents know that they are important too.
D. Dress in pajamas. The group does not care what an employee wears as long as their presentation is good.

16. Professionally, what is the longest it should take someone to respond to a resident's email? How about a phone call?
    A. 45 minutes; 15 minutes
    B. 24 hours; 24 hours
    C. 48 hours; 24 hours
    D. 24 hours; 4 hours

16.____

17. Unlike social etiquette, office and business professionalism are PRIMARILY based on
    A. hierarchy and power
    B. personal relations between employees and customers
    C. common sense and courtesy
    D. both A and C

17.____

18. If something goes wrong during interaction with or presentation for a local community group, what should you do?
    A. Clear your head, focus, and be cheerful and professional and act like nothing went wrong
    B. Take responsibility and take appropriate action
    C. Blame others for your technical difficulties
    D. Find a way to end the interaction as quickly as possible

18.____

19. What is the ultimate goal of customer service?
    A. Customer satisfaction
    B. Understanding customers
    C. Identify problems
    D. Improve product and service

19.____

20. Of the following, which is the BEST reason for office employees and supervisors to frequently gauge customer satisfaction?
    A. No reason. One evaluation is enough.
    B. Because employees are not always honest about reporting customer satisfaction.
    C. They may have concerns or complaints that they have not voiced.
    D. Complaints do not always reach management.

20.____

21. Which of the following is TRUE of scope of influence?
    A. It is objective.
    B. Some have a larger scope of influence than others.
    C. Everyone has the same scope of influence.
    D. It is not relevant to customer service.

21.____

22. Which of the following techniques will create credibility in the minds of local residents in regards to their government representatives?
    A. Never admit being wrong. It undermines credibility.
    B. Demonstrate your human emotions. Whether you're angry or happy, let others see it.

22.____

C. Tell people what they want to hear even if it is not necessarily what you know to be true.
D. Become an expert about various factors in your profession. People will respect your knowledge.

23. You are in a "train the trainer" meeting about meeting customer expectations. As you talk in small groups after a short presentation, four people express very different statements about customer expectations.
Which one is CORRECT?
A. "Wrong. Customer expectations are always changing."
B. "Customer expectations rarely change."
C. "Guys, all you really have to do is make a promise to solve customer problems. They forget after a while, even if you don't follow through."
D. "Do not worry about what other companies are doing. We should focus on ourselves."

23.____

24. Of the following, which of the following is TRUE concerning customer service?
A. Average customer service will always suffice.
B. Customers lost through poor customer service are easy to replace.
C. Organizations must provide excellent customer service or expect failure.
D. None of the above

24.____

25. You are in a tense conversation with a very upset and aggressive resident. How should you handle this situation?
A. Make them respect and value your time.
B. Avoid admitting any wrongdoing on your part.
C. Find a solution and implement it.
D. Do not show empathy.

25.____

KEY (CORRECT ANSWERS)

1. D
2. B
3. C
4. A
5. B

6. A
7. C
8. D
9. C
10. D

11. A
12. B
13. C
14. A
15. B

16. D
17. D
18. B
19. A
20. C

21. B
22. D
23. A
24. C
25. C

EXAMINATION SECTION
TEST 1

DIRECTIONS: Each question or incomplete statement is followed by several suggested answers or completions. Select the one that BEST answers the question or completes the statement. *PRINT THE LETTER OF THE CORRECT ANSWER IN THE SPACE AT THE RIGHT.*

1. Notice of an injury or death for which compensation is payable shall be given to the employer within _____ days after the accident causing such injury.
   A. 15   B. 30   C. 45   D. 60

2. "Disability" means the state of being disabled from earning _____ wages at the work at which the employee was last employed.
   A. half   B. partial   C. substantive   D. full

3. Daniel began his employment as a dispatcher at the ABC Bus Corp., a coach bus company based in Rochester, in 2007. During a scheduled fire drill, Daniel fell from the dispatch booth and severely injured his right knee. During Daniel's knee operation, he contracted a blood-borne disease.
   Which of the following is ABC Bus Corp.'s BEST defense against liability?
   A. Daniel did not contract a disease as a result of his employment as a dispatcher.
   B. Daniel would likely have needed knee surgery in his lifetime.
   C. Daniel should not have participated in the mandatory fire drill for all employees.
   D. Daniel should have been more careful in exiting the dispatch booth during the fire drill.

4. Sarah learns from her new hire orientation that generally compensation is not allowed for the first _____ day after injury. However, in cases where the injury results in disability of more than _____ days, compensation shall be allowed from the date of the disability.
   A. 3; 14   B. 7; 14   C. 10; 14   D. 14; 14

5. James is injured while unloading boxes at a local grocery store. The grocery store owner, Matthew, pays James in cash each week to unload deliveries that arrive at the store after 10 P.M. since no other store employees are available at that time. James is not on the payroll of the grocery store.
   Will the grocery store be liable for James' injuries?
   A. Yes, because he was working on the store's behalf at the time of the injury.
   B. Yes, because James can prove his injuries are related to his job duties.
   C. Yes, because James is an eligible person under the Workers' Compensation laws.
   D. No, because James is not a covered employee of the grocery store.

2 (#1)

Questions 6-7.

DIRECTIONS: Questions 6 and 7 are to be answered on the basis of the following fact pattern.

David and his friend, Bruce, are in the healthcare business. David is a healthcare attorney and works for a local clinic. Bruce is a chiropractor in the hospital where David is employed.

6. Bruce asks David for a list of individuals who have visited the hospital based on Workers Compensation claims. David provides it, not knowing Bruce will use it to solicit business to the chiropractor unit. Bruce then continues to seek out individuals injured during their course of their employment.
   May Bruce continue this practice?
   A. Yes, as long as he treats patients who are legitimately injured.
   B. Yes, as long as he treats patients who were legitimately injured while at work.
   C. No, because Bruce cannot prove the patients are eligible for Workers' Compensation coverage.
   D. No, because Bruce is prohibited from soliciting Workers' Compensation business in this manner.

6._____

7. If Bruce were guilty of a crime, what would the crime be classified as?
   A. Felony
   B. Misdemeanor
   C. Infraction
   D. Violation

7._____

Questions 8-10.

DIRECTIONS: Questions 8 through 10 are to be answered on the basis of the following fact pattern.

Orange, Inc. receives a bill from the Oakdale Hospital for medical treatment provided to one of their employees, Bill. Bill was injured nearly one month ago.

8. How many days does Orange, Inc. have to pay the bill to Oakdale Hospital?
   A. 15   B. 30   C. 45   D. 60

8._____

9. If Orange, Inc. decides not to pay the bill from Oakdale Hospital, what action must the company take?
   A. Notify the hospital and explain the reason for non-payment
   B. Notify the hospital and Bill in writing that the bill will not be paid
   C. Notify Bill, but not the hospital, that the bill will not be paid
   D. Record the non-payment as a liability in the company books and records

9._____

10. Assume that there is a dispute as to the value of the services rendered. If Oakdale Hospital requests, the dispute will be decided by which method of dispute resolution?
    A. Mediation   B. Arbitration   C. Litigation   D. Transaction

10._____

11. Which of the following procedures must Jill submit to after she is injured at work?
    A. Process of review of Jill's salary history
    B. An employment review to ensure she is a full-time employee
    C. Physical examination
    D. Familial review

    11.____

12. The injured employee or his dependents, if so requested, shall furnish the last employer or the board with such information as to the names and addresses of all his other employers during the last _____ months.
    A. six   B. eight   C. twelve   D. eighteen

    12.____

Questions 13-14.

DIRECTIONS: Questions 13 and 14 are to be answered on the basis of the following fact pattern.

Adam submits that he injured his right knee at work. He tells his employer that the bathroom floor was slippery and he fell forward, and now cannot work. Adam completes paperwork to the same effect and submits to the Workers' Compensation Board. Adam really injured himself at home in the shower.

13. What crime is Adam guilty of?
    Offering a false
    A. written statement
    B. instrument for filing in the first degree
    C. instrument as a misdemeanor
    D. application

    13.____

14. What classification is the crime that Adam committed?
    A. Infraction   B. Violation
    C. Misdemeanor   D. Class E felony

    14.____

15. While at work, Anthony loses his balance and falls on a slippery bathroom floor. There was a sign that the floor was slippery. Anthony hurt his right shoulder and right hip in the fall. Anthony previously fell at the office under similar circumstances. He submits an application for Workers' Compensation insurance.
    Has Anthony committed a crime?
    A. Yes, he is guilty of a Class A Felony.
    B. Yes, he is guilty of a Class C Felony.
    C. No, because there was a sign that the floor was slippery.
    D. No, because no crime was committed; it is possible Anthony was injured twice at the same job.

    15.____

16. Which of the following is an employer required to maintain as part of their payroll records?
    A. Number of employees   B. Classification of employees
    C. Record of employee accidents D. All of the above

    16.____

4 (#1)

17. The administrative head of the Workers Compensation Board is also known as the   17.____
    A. Director   B. Executive Director
    C. Chair   D. Chief

Questions 18-20.

DIRECTIONS: Questions 18 through 20 are to be answered on the basis of the following fact pattern.

After Diana is injured at work, she informs her immediate supervisor of her injuries and schedules a meeting with her employer's Human Resource Department. She is told to go home and that Workers Compensation benefits would "kick in immediately". Diana continues to call into work to check on the status of her benefits. She is told she does not need to fill out any paperwork and to simply wait for her employer to contact her. Diana does not return to work for one month and is subsequently terminated.

18. Diana's employer has likely committed which of the following?   18.____
    A. Non-compliance or default
    B. Restitution of benefits
    C. Diana's employer is not liable for any wrongdoing
    D. Diana was rightfully terminated for insubordination

19. Assume that Diana earned $100,000 per year at her job. Diana's employer is liable to pay which amount?   19.____
    A. $120 or the sum so expended, pursuant to Section 213
    B. $10,000 or the sum so expended, pursuant to Section 213
    C. Diana's employer is not liable for any amount
    D. Diana's employer is not liable for any amount greater than 1% of Diana's total wages

20. The head of the Human Resource Department realizes the error in handling Diana's situation and calls Diana at home to explain the process for filing for Workers Compensation benefits. The initial Human Resource representative was misinformed and it was his first day on the job.   20.____
    The actions of Diana's employer during her first visit with Human Resources was likely
    A. purposeful   B. extravagant   C. inadvertent   D. uneventful

21. Any employer who fails to make provisions for payment of disability or family leave benefits as required within _____ days shall be guilty of a misdemeanor and upon conviction be punishable by a fine of not less than _____ nor more than five hundred dollars or imprisonment for not more than one year or both.   21.____
    A. 10; $100   B. 15; $100   C. 20; $150   D. 20; $200

22. Any person who has previously been convicted of a failure to make provisions for payment of disability or family leave benefits within the preceding five years, upon conviction for a second violation such person shall be fined no more than _____ in addition to any other penalties including fines otherwise provided by law.
    A. $500   B. $1,250   C. $2,500   D. $5,000

Questions 23-25.

DIRECTIONS: Questions 23 through 25 are to be answered on the basis of the following fact pattern.

Acme Corporation has posted noticed around the workplace that state the company has provided for the payment of disability and family leave benefits as provided by law.

23. There are two kitchens located at Acme Headquarters in Rochester. Assume that Acme has posted the notices inside the kitchen pantry doors.
    The law requires that the notices be posted in
    A. company eateries
    B. within 10 yards of an employee's workstation
    C. conspicuous places
    D. at eye level

24. The Head of the Workers Compensation Board has requested a written statement from Acme showing the manner in which the company has complied with the notice requirement.
    How long does Acme have to furnish this letter?
    A. 10 days   B. 30 days   C. 90 days   D. 95 days

25. Failure to furnish such written statement shall constitute _____ that such employer has neglected or failed in respect of an of the matters so required.
    A. exclusive right   B. inconclusive evidence
    C. presumptive evidence   D. uncontroverted evidence

KEY (CORRECT ANSWERS)

1.	B	11.	C
2.	D	12.	C
3.	A	13.	B
4.	B	14.	D
5.	D	15.	D
6.	D	16.	D
7.	B	17.	C
8.	C	18.	A
9.	A	19.	A
10.	B	20.	C

21. A
22. B
23. C
24. A
25. C

TEST 2

DIRECTIONS: Each question or incomplete statement is followed by several suggested answers or completions. Select the one that BEST answers the question or completes the statement. *PRINT THE LETTER OF THE CORRECT ANSWER IN THE SPACE AT THE RIGHT.*

Questions 1-3.

DIRECTIONS: Questions 1 through 3 are to be answered on the basis of the following fact pattern.

Bryan had a pre-existing muscle condition when he began his job as a delivery driver for a local shipping company. Due to his condition, he needed to take three half-hour breaks during each eight hour shift (in addition to his lunch break). While taking one of his scheduled breaks, Bryan slipped in the company breakroom and broke his leg. He filed for Workers' Compensation shortly thereafter.

1. Bryan's employer has asked for Bryan's Workers Compensation record from the Workers' Compensation Board, believing that Bryan may be fraudulently procuring benefits.
   May the Workers Compensation Board furnish Bryan's report?
   A. Yes, if the request is furnished in written, rather than oral, format
   B. Yes, if the employer is Bryan's only employer in the preceding eight months before the accident
   C. Yes, if Bryan's employer has a legitimate reason for requesting such documents and record
   D. No

2. Assume that Bryan's employer later sues Bryan for fraud, extortion, and libel. Assume that Bryan countersues for negligence. Bryan's attorney has requested Bryan's Workers Compensation record from the Board, pursuant to a subpoena.
   May the Workers Compensation Board furnish Bryan's records in this instance?
   A. Yes
   B. No, because Bryan's attorney does not have a legitimate reason
   C. No, because Bryan has filed a countersuit
   D. No, because the Board may only furnish records to Bryan's employer

3. During the legal proceedings, Bryan asserts that he never saw any posting or notice that his employer furnishes payment of disability and family leave benefits. Bryan's employer alleges that such notices were placed in _____ places all around the company, including in the breakroom where Bryan fell.
   A. luminous   B. conspicuous   C. accessible   D. terminal

2 (#2)

4. The head of a state or municipal department, board, commission or office authorized or required by law to issue any permit for work involving the employment of employees in a hazardous job shall not issue such permit unless proof of _____ is secured.
   A. compensation for all employees by an insurance carrier
   B. proper accounting records capability
   C. proper and discrete records capability
   D. documentation of all employee names, ages, and pre-existing health conditions

4._____

5. Bill is a contractor who completes home inspections for hazardous materials in the Suffolk County area. Bill subcontracts some of his work to his nephew, Jared, when he is unavailable. Jared contracts mesothelioma in his work for his uncle.
   Who is liable and must pay for compensation to Jared?
   A. The homeowners who had asbestos
   B. Bill
   C. Jared
   D. No one is liable as mesothelioma is airborne

5._____

6. Cathy is injured at work on July 1. When will she likely receive her first Workers Compensation payment?
   A. July 8   B. July 15   C. July 20   D. July 30

6._____

7. Which of the following is a category of disability?
   A. Permanent total disability   B. Temporary total disability
   C. Permanent partial disability   D. All of the above

7._____

8. In the case of disability, a _____ is followed that allows for adjustment based on the category of disability and/or the applicable disfigurement.
   A. remuneration   B. schedule   C. example   D. retreat

8._____

9. James has lost the use of his right thumb after his hand was caught in a piece of machinery at work.
   How is James compensated for the permanent total loss of use of his right thumb?
   James is compensated
   A. as if he lost his right thumb   B. as if he lost two digits
   C. for a temporary total disability   D. as if he lost three digits

9._____

10. Pursuant to Article 2 of the Workers' Compensation Law, in case where an injury results in disability of more than fourteen days, compensation is allowed from what date?
    A. Date of filing for benefits
    B. Date of disability
    C. Date of employer recognition of disability
    D. Thirty days after the onset of disability

10._____

3 (#2)

11. In the case of death, Workers Compensation benefits are deemed _____ benefits. 11._____
    A. inheritance   B. excise   C. related   D. death

12. Notice of an injury or death for which compensation shall be given within _____ days after the accident causing such injury, and also in case of the death of the employee resulting from such injury, within _____ days after such death. 12._____
    A. 15; 30   B. 30; 30   C. 30; 45   D. 30; 60

Questions 13-16.

DIRECTIONS: Questions 13 through 16 are to be answered on the basis of the following fact pattern.

A crane that Joe was operating at work fell on him, killing him instantly. Joe is predeceased by his wife, Susan, and his adult son, Bob.

13. Notice of Joe's death must be relayed to which party? 13._____
    A. Joe's employer
    B. The crane operator
    C. The chair of the Workers Compensation Board directly
    D. Joe's insurance carrier

14. Which of the following is NOT required to be included in the notice? 14._____
    A. Name of the employee
    B. Time, place, nature of the injury
    C. The address of the employee
    D. The gender and age of the employee

15. What is the result of a failure to provide such notice? 15._____
    A. Bar to any claim under Workers Compensation laws
    B. Delay in payment of claims
    C. Bar to surviving spouse insurance allowable under Article 2
    D. Bar to additional fringe benefits offered by the employer prior to the death of the employee

16. Which of the following parties is eligible to provide the notice? 16._____
    A. Joe's co-workers
    B. Only Joe's co-workers that were present at the accident scene
    C. Susan
    D. Bob's wife, Jill

4 (#2)

Questions 17-19.

DIRECTIONS: Questions 17 through 19 are to be answered on the basis of the following fact pattern.

Jamal is awarded $125 per week in Workers Compensation benefits, stemming from an injury to his left foot that occurred while Jamal was working as a personal driver in New York City.

17. Is Jamal eligible to appeal the award?   17.____
    A. No, because Jamal is still able to work
    B. No, because Jamal is not totally disabled or suffering from a permanent loss of use of his left foot
    C. Yes, because Jamal is a personal driver
    D. Yes

18. Assuming that Jamal is eligible to appeal, how many days does Jamal have to file an appeal and from what date does that period begin?   18.____
    A. Ten days after notice of filing of an award
    B. Fifteen days after commencement of the board
    C. Thirty days after notice of filing of an award
    D. Thirty days after commencement of the board

19. An award or decision of the board contains which of the following?   19.____
    A. Statement of the facts which formed the basis of the Board's action
    B. The issues raised before it on such application
    C. A statement that the award is final and conclusive
    D. All of the above

Questions 20-22.

DIRECTIONS: Questions 20 through 22 are to be answered on the basis of the following fact pattern.

Bird Consulting, Inc. hired several consultants to map bird populations in the greater New York City area. Bird Consulting, Inc. also hired three full-time employees, Abe, Bill, and Carl, to assist in office administration tasks.

20. One of the consultants, Rich, is injured while surveying an area in Brooklyn. Rich was recording a flock of birds flying above the Gowanus Canal and accidently fell into the canal, injuring his ribs.   20.____
    Is Rich entitled to Workers Compensation benefits?
    A. No, because he is not a covered employee
    B. No, because the activity engaged in is inherently dangerous
    C. Yes, because Rich is an employee of Bird Consulting
    D. Yes, because Rich was working at the time of the accident

21. Carl is asked by one of his managers to move 50-pound boxes from the warehouse into the office. Carl injures his back while completing this task and files for Workers Compensation benefits.
    When will Carl receive his first benefit check?
    A. One month after the accident
    B. Seven days after the accident
    C. Forty days after the accident
    D. The accident is not covered

    21.____

22. In an effort to delay payment of Carl's benefits, Bird Consulting files an application to the Workers Compensation Board to modify Carl's award.
    What is the fine for interfering with the payment of compensation to Carl?
    A. $100
    B. $200
    C. $500
    D. $1,000

    22.____

Questions 23-25.

DIRECTIONS: Questions 23 through 25 are to be answered on the basis of the following fact pattern.

Jamie is desperate for a job. He interviews with a small law firm who wants to hire him but cannot afford his services. The law firm manager indicates that they would be happy to hire Jamie, but would not be able to provide him with any benefits.

23. Jamie offers to pay for his own Workers' Compensation benefits.
    May an employee agree to pay a portion of the premium required by his or her employer to the state insurance fund?
    A. Yes, if the agreement is in writing
    B. Yes if there is a meeting of the minds between the parties
    C. Yes, if the employer willingly participates in the contract and makes timely payments
    D. No, an agreement of this nature is invalid

    23.____

24. If the law firm hired Jamie and accepted his payments—in the form of a direct deduction from Jamie's paycheck—what, if any, punishment will be imposed?
    A. No punishment is imposed as it is a lawful transaction.
    B. No punishment is imposed as the payment is deducted directly from Jamie's paycheck.
    C. The law firm will need to pay a small fine to the Workers Compensation Board.
    D. The law firm shall be guilty of a misdemeanor.

    24.____

25. Instead of an agreement to pay a portion of the Workers' Compensation premiums, Jamie offers to waive his right to Workers' Compensation.
    Is this waiver agreement valid?
    A. Yes, if executed in writing
    B. Yes, as long as Jamie is fully apprised of the inherit risk in such an agreement
    C. Yes, if Jamie provided proof of other insurance that affords him similar protections

    25.____

KEY (CORRECT ANSWERS)

1.	D	11.	D
2.	A	12.	B
3.	B	13.	A
4.	A	14.	D
5.	B	15.	A
6.	A	16.	C
7.	D	17.	D
8.	B	18.	C
9.	A	19.	D
10.	B	20.	A

21. B
22. C
23. D
24. D
25. D

EXAMINATION SECTION
TEST 1

DIRECTIONS: Each question or incomplete statement is followed by several suggested answers or completions. Select the one that BEST answers the question or completes the statement. *PRINT THE LETTER OF THE CORRECT ANSWER IN THE SPACE AT THE RIGHT.*

1. The following passage is taken from the Workers' Compensation Provisions of the Consolidated Laws of New York State:
 § 238. *Payments to minors. Minors shall be deemed to be sui juris for the purpose of receiving payment of benefits under this article.*
 This passage means that minor employees

   A. are a unique class of employees whose cases should be considered using a different set of standards
   B. must be represented by a parent or guardian in workers' compensation cases
   C. will be compensated in the same way as any other worker who is eligible for workers' compensation
   D. must designate an adult who will nominally receive benefits and then transfer them to the minor

2. The purpose of a partial disability benefit is to

   A. allow the insured to collect full benefits during rehabilitation
   B. protect the insurer against material misrepresentation
   C. protect the insurer against adverse selection
   D. provide reduced monthly indemnity in proportion to the insured's loss of income when he/she has returned to work at reduced earnings

3. Fred has been totally disabled by a work-related injury for 415 weeks. Fred's injury has been identified as a 32 percent whole-body impairment. Under the workers' compensation system, the maximum benefit rate is .6667. Fred's average weekly wage is $378.80. The total amount of benefits received by Fred over the 415-week period is about

   A. $33,538
   B. $50,305
   C. $104,808
   D. $157,202

4. When a workers' compensation case has been refiled, with a notation that an examiner is to review the case by a specified future date, the case has said to be in

   A. apportionment
   B. abeyance
   C. reopening
   D. escrow

5. A worker has been continuously disabled for more than two years. Under many private or self-insurance plans, the insurer can request proof of continued disability no more frequently than once every

A. three years
B. eighteen months
C. six months
D. 90 days

6. An employee injured while traveling to or from work is generally NOT covered by workers compensation if he
   I. is simply driving to or from the workplace
   II. engages in a work-related task during the trip to or from work
   III. is paid for travel time
   IV. is provided transportation by the employer

   A. I only
   B. I or II
   C. II or III
   D. I, II, III or IV

7. Which of the following would LEAST likely be considered a work-related injury under federal guidelines?

   A. Sharon, a data entry clerk, falls when getting out of her car before beginning work.
   B. John, a chef, slips and falls while at work in the kitchen.
   C. Cliff, a custodial worker, is stung by a yellowjacket in the maintenance yard and has an allergic reaction.
   D. Mary, a salesperson, is injured in a car accident on her way to see her employer's client as part of her regular duties.

8. The indemnity for total disability generally is written on a _____.

   A. service
   B. flat
   C. reimbursement
   D. valued

9. The first part of a disability rating is the

   A. impairment number
   B. impairment standard
   C. occupational grouping
   D. age adjustment

10. Each of the following is a condition that constitutes presumptive disability, EXCEPT:

    A. loss of the use of any limb
    B. loss of sight in both eyes
    C. loss of hearing in both ears
    D. the loss of power of speech

11. When an employee is judged by a physician to have attained maximum medical improvement (MMI), he or she
    I. is no longer eligible for workers' compensation benefits
    II. has recovered from the work injury to the greatest extent that is expected
    III. expects no further change in his or her condition
    IV. is automatically considered to be partially disabled

    A. I only
    B. I and II
    C. II and III
    D. I, II, III and IV

11.____

12. Customer service at any agency is a matter of both style and substance. The "substance" of customer service at a workers compensation division or department would include each of the following, EXCEPT

    A. friendliness and approachability
    B. problem-solving skills
    C. knowledge of state laws and regulations
    D. knowledge about agency procedures

12.____

13. The federal _____ assigns private employers the duty to provide a workplace free of hazards that may cause death or serious harm.

    A. Fair Labor Standards
    B. Occupational Safety and Health
    C. Employees' Compensation
    D. Robinson-Patman

13.____

14. Under the ADA, employers may be required to make changes in the workplace or to a job description in response to the needs of an otherwise qualified employee or candidate with a disability. These changes are referred to as

    A. rehabilitative employment
    B. work modification
    C. accessibility measures
    D. reasonable accommodations

14.____

Questions 15 and 16 are based on the information below:

In certain industrial categories, a state workers' compensation system uses a tiered benefit system, calculating total disability benefits according to an employee's years of service at the time a disability due to illness or injury begins. An employee with 10 or more years of service receives 100 percent of his or her base salary, for up to 26 weeks. An employee with fewer than 10 years of service receives 100 percent of his or her base salary for up to the first 4 weeks (28 days). After those first four weeks, the benefit drops to 90 percent for up to the next 9 weeks (63 days); and after that the benefit is 75 percent for up to the next 13 weeks (91 days).
Ruth Brynner, who is covered under this provision, has worked at the same company for 8 years. She is injured on the job and is totally disabled, unable to return to work for 3 months, or 12 weeks. Her base salary at the time she was injured was $65,000 per year (52 weeks).

15. The total amount of benefits received by Ruth Brynner during her 4 months of total disability was

15.____

A. $12,000
B. $13,500
C. $14,000
D. $15,000

16. Gerald Simpson, who is also covered under the above provisions, has worked at the same company for five years. He is injured on the job, totally disabled, and unable to return to work for 6 months, or 24 weeks. His base salary at the time of his injury was $52,000 per year.
The total amount of benefits earned by Gerald Simpson during his 6 months of total disability was

A. $18,000
B. $20,350
C. $21,250
D. $24,000

16.___

17. Workers compensation benefits generally include payments for
   I. lost wages/lost time
   II. medical services
   III. rehabilitation services
   IV. death benefits

A. I and II
B. I, II and IV
C. I and IV
D. I, II, III and IV

17.___

18. Many workers' compensation insurers adjust premiums by adding loss reserves for estimated future claims costs to paid losses. This is a concept known as _____.

A. indirect
B. partial
C. earned
D. incurred

18.___

19. _____ are NOT typically covered under workers' compensation laws.

A. Service
B. Industrial
C. Government
D. Agricultural

19.___

20. Tim works twenty hours a week at Acme Leasing at $8 an hour, and works twenty hours a week for Bob's Country Bunker at $10) an hour. Tim is injured while working for Acme leasing. Tim's average weekly wage is calculated by multiplying the total number of hours he works in a five-day work week, regardless of his employer, by the wage he was paid at the job at which he was injured.
Tim's average weekly wage is

A. $160
B. $200

20.___

C. $320
D. $400

21. According to the U.S. Chamber of Commerce, six basic objectives underlie workers' compensation laws. Which of the following is NOT one of them?

    A. To discourage injured workers from returning to work to soon after they have suffered an injury or illness.
    B. To provide a single remedy that reduces court delays, costs and workloads arising from personal injury litigation.
    C. To encourage maximum employer interest in safety and rehabilitation through experience-rating mechanisms.
    D. To relieve public and private charities of financial drains incident to uncompensated industrial accidents.

21.____

22. In the state where Bob works, employees are entitled to workers' compensation benefits up to two-thirds of their average weekly wage, within the minimum and maximum amounts allowed by law. Bob is injured at work on June 5, 2007, and is assigned a 50 percent disability rating. The maximum average weekly amount allowed for an injury occurring in 2007 is $180 for a partial disability rating under 15 percent; $220 for a PD rating from 15 to 24.75 percent; $250 for a PD rating from 25 to 69.75 percent; and $280 for a PD rating of 70 percent or higher. Bob's average weekly wage at his job is $600. He is entitled to a maximum benefit amount of

    A. $250
    B. $280
    C. $400
    D. $600

22.____

23. Which of the following is an occupational disease that is caused by continuous trauma?

    A. Chemical burn
    B. Radiation sickness
    C. Carpal-tunnel syndrome
    D. Silicosis

23.____

24. Steve Stephens is a clerk for the U.S. Postal Service. One day at the office, Steve opens the top drawer of a filing cabinet, and the entire cabinet suddenly falls over on top of him. His left arm is broken, as well as several bones in his left foot. Which of the following describes the mechanism by which Steve can recover benefits for his injuries?

    A. Steve will receive payment for his lost time and medical expenses under the Nonappropriated Fund Instrumentalities Act.
    B. The Federal Employers' Liability Act allows Steve to sue his employer if his injuries resulted from the employer's negligence.
    C. Steve will receive payment for his lost time and medical expenses under the state workers' compensation system
    D. The Federal Employees' Compensation Act entitles Steve to receive workers' compensation benefits.

24.____

25. If a worker is partially disabled, the benefit is payable as follows:

    $$\frac{A-B}{A} \times \text{weekly benefit for total disability}$$

    where:
    A = the worker's pre-claim weekly earnings
    B = the worker's weekly earnings for work in which partial disability is claimed

    Apply this formula to the following problem: Jared Hass's salary is $40,000 annually. After six years of service to Clomp Corporation, Hass is injured on the job and becomes totally disabled, earning a weekly benefit that is 75 percent of his previous salary. After several weeks, Hass returns to work on a part-time basis, earning $250 a week. His partial disability benefit will be about

    A. $154
    B. $250
    C. $389
    D. $519

KEY (CORRECT ANSWERS)

1. C	11. C
2. D	12. A
3. A	13. B
4. B	14. D
5. C	15. C
6. A	16. B
7. A	17. D
8. D	18. D
9. A	19. D
10. A	20. C

21. A
22. A
23. C
24. D
25. C

TEST 2

DIRECTIONS: Each question or incomplete statement is followed by several suggested answers or completions. Select the one that BEST answers the question or completes the statement. *PRINT THE LETTER OF THE CORRECT ANSWER IN THE SPACE AT THE RIGHT.*

Questions 1 and 2 refer to the information below:

In the state where Edna works, partial dependents are entitled to death benefits-four times the amount annually devoted to their respective levels of support by the deceased employee. The total benefit divided by the partial dependents, however, cannot exceed $125,000; if it does, the dependents will divide a proportionate share of the maximum.

Edna partially supported her three college-aged children: Matt received $15,000 a year from her; Carl received $7,000 annually, and Dorothy received $5,000. Edna was killed in an injury at work in October of 2000.

1. What was the death benefit received by Carl?

    A. $7,000
    B. $28,000
    C. $32,500
    D. $65,000

2. What was the total benefit received by Edna's children?

    A. $65,000
    B. $94,000
    C. $108,000
    D. $125,000

3. Questions of work-relatedness arise in situations where an employee is injured while attending to personal matters on company time. In terms of a compensation claim's validity, the most important factor to consider in these situations would be

    A. whether the employer had a suited policy of allowing employees to engage in personal activities while on the job
    B. whether the employer was aware that the employee was attending to personal matters on company time
    C. whether the employee had "punched in" for the day
    D. whether the personal matter could have been considered an emergency

4. Of the following, the most common cause of workers' compensation overcharge is

    A. incorrect scheduling of injury
    B. claimant fraud
    C. incorrect job classification code
    D. employer fraud

5. Generally, employees covered by workers compensation may not sue employers for injuries suffered in the course of their employment. Possible exceptions to this rule would include the case of
    I. John, who is assaulted by his employer during a disagreement
    II. Mary, who is injured while a passenger in her employer's car on a sales call. The accident is found largely to have been caused by the employer's speed, which was in excess of 100 miles per hour.
    III. Hank, who is injured on the job but believes his job has been misclassified by his employer in order to avoid a higher pre mium.
    IV. Ellen, a delivery assistant who is injured in the course of a delivery when a truck driven by her employer rearends the car in front of it

    A. I and II
    B. I, II, and III
    C. I and IV
    D. I, II, III and IV

6. Jerry does data entry at a computer terminal all day long. He notices pain in his right wrist and sees his family doctor, who does some testing. Jerry's doctor tells him that he has carpal tunnel syndrome, caused by his constant typing at the computer terminal at work. Jerry continues to work for another three months before finally telling his supervisor he can't work any more because of the caipal tunnel syndrome and going home. In his state, Jerry has one year from the "date of injury" to file a workers' compensation claim. For this purpose, the "date of injury" would be the day

    A. Jerry first felt pain in his right wrist
    B. the pain in Jerry's right wrist affected his work productivity
    C. Jerry's doctor told him he had carpal tunnel syndrome due to work
    D. Jerry informed his employer of the doctor's diagnosis and took off work

7. The requirements for a valid workers' compensation claim in most jurisdictions state that in order for an injury to be compensable, it must occur
    I. when the employee is actively engaged in his job
    II. while the employee is fulfilling work duties
    III. within the precise work hours prescribed by the employer.
    IV. in a location where it is reasonable for the employee to be while working

    A. I and III
    B. II and IV
    C. II, III and IV
    D. I, II, III and IV

8. Typically, partial disability is NOT

    A. insured so that benefits will encourage the insured to return to work on a limited basis during the convalescent period
    B. a condition that follows a period of total disability, if sickness is the cause
    C. defined as the inability to perform one or more important duties of the insured's regular occupation
    D. awarded the same amount as a total disability, but for a shorter period of time

9. Which of the following accurately describes a factor that affects the length of a temporary disability?

A. Blue collar workers, because of their strong cultural work ethic, tend to have relatively shorter periods of temporary disability.
B. Younger workers, because of their lack of caution, tend to suffer injuries that take longer to heal.
C. The claimant may be motivated to prolong the period of disability when a claim is in litigation.
D. Office workers often have an adversarial relationship with their employer that discourages a prompt return to work.

10. Which of the following would NOT be considered a "third party" in a workers compensation claim?   10.____

    A. The manufacturer of a defective product that injured the worker.
    B. The co-worker who accidentally injured the worker
    C. A property owner (not the employer) who failed to properly maintain a safe workplace.
    D. The owner of an animal that bit a worker.

11. Luther is on the steps of his employer's premises when he slips and sprains his ankle. He   11.____
    is taken to the employers' infirmary, where his ankle is iced down, and he is able to return to his desk for work within an hour. He is sore but feels fine otherwise. Which of the following is true?

    A. The accident must be reported to the employer and the workers' compensation agency.
    B. The accident must be reported to the employer and the workers' compensation agency only if it interferes with or affects Luther's ability to work.
    C. The accident should only be reported if Luther was actively engaged in his job
    D. Because Luther was not hospitalized and did not miss a significant amount of work, the accident does not need to be reported.

12. The following passage is from the California Labor Code: 12.____

    3501. (a) A child under the age of 18 years, or a child of any age found by any trier of fact, whether contractual, administrative, regulatory, or judicial, to be physically or mentally incapacitated from earning, shall be conclusively presumed to be wholly dependent for support upon a deceased employee-parent with whom that child is living at the time of injury resulting in death of the parent or for whose maintenance the parent was legally liable at the time of injury resulting in death of the parent, there being no surviving totally dependent parent.
    (b) A spouse to whom a deceased employee is married at the lime of death shall be conclusively presumed to be wholly dependent for support upon the deceased employee if the surviving spouse earned thirty thousand dollars ($30,000) or less in the twelve months immediately preceding the death.
    John, a worker at a Los Angeles foundry, is killed in an accident. His wife, Imelda, is a teacher whose salary is $50,00(3 a year. John and Imelda have three children: Rose, 15 years old; Vincent, 13, and Jennifer, 10. John's son from a previous marriage, Brent, is 19 and lives in the same household.
    Based on the above excerpt from the labor code, how many members of John's household could be considered "total dependents?"

A. 0
B. 1
C. 3
D. 4

13. A worker has an average weekly wage of $1000, which in her state qualifies her for a $600 weekly maximum disability benefit. As a result of a work-related accident, the worker's income was reduced to an average of $700 for several weeks after the accident. Under the workers' compensation plan, a weekly disability benefit is equal to the percentage of income lost as a result of sickness or accident multiplied by the maximum weekly disability benefit. In this case, the worker's average weekly benefit would be 13._____

   A. $60
   B. $180
   C. $200
   D. $300

14. In most jurisdictions, newer disability rating schedules allow physicians to rely on _____ the purpose of calculating a rating. 14._____
      I.   objective findings
      II. subjective complaints by the employee, such as pain
      III. work restrictions

   A. I only
   B. I and II
   C. I and III
   D. I, II and III

15. Disputes or disagreements over benefit entitlement can occur at any time in the life of a workers' compensation claim and can arise over any issue. Which of the following is LEAST likely to be one of these issues? 15._____

   A. extent of permanent partial disability or entitlement to ongoing wage-loss benefits
   B. whether the client is truly sick or injured
   C. whether the current disability is related to the work-related injury or disease
   D. entitlement to permanent total disability benefits and, if entitled, for how much and how long

16. The most common type of workers' compensation claim is caused by 16._____

   A. a long-brewing situation that has reached a "breaking point"
   B. a sudden and unexpected occurrence
   C. a fairly long and unsuccessful treatment regimen
   D. employee dissatisfaction

17. Which of the following is NOT an approach used to settle a workers' compensation claim? 17._____

   A. Public hearing
   B. Direct Settlement
   C. Union arbitration
   D. Agreement settlement

5 (#2)

18. In California, a payment that has been unreasonably delayed or refused by an insurer is subject to a penalty of 25 percent or $10,000, whichever is less.

    Herman does not get his disability check in the amount of $340 until four weeks past the date it is due. For this period, if the insurer's delay is found to be unreasonable, Herman's insurer owes him a total of

    A. $85
    B. $255
    C. $340
    D. $425

    18.____

19. An employer who has been authorized by the appropriate agency to administer and pay directly on employee compensation claims is described as

    A. self-insured
    B. immune from action
    C. in compliance
    D. pre-qualified

    19.____

20. Common reasons for an employee's challenge of an assigned disability rating include

    I. wrong occupation or occupational group
    II. wrong work restrictions given by physician
    III. incomplete or inaccurate medical history used by the treating doctor
    IV. age was not taken correctly into account

    A. I and II
    B. II and III
    C. III and IV
    D. I, II, III and IV

    20.____

21. The _____ of some workers compensation programs is payable in the event of accidental death and, in some cases, accidental dismemberment.

    A. total disability
    B. flatline
    C. whole life
    D. principal sum

    21.____

22. A visibly upset claimant asks an examiner to index her claim, even though the required medical forms have not yet been received at the department, because she desperately needs her benefit to be paid in order to pay for child care. The claimant assures the examiner that her physician has said she will qualify for a total temporary disability benefit and that the report can simply be slipped into the file after it is put into the system. Instead of directly saying "no" to the claimant, the examiner would MOST effectively begin her response by saying:

    A. "Here's what we can do to get your claim moving through the system as quickly as possible."
    B. "Even if your claim were filed, I couldn't simply hand you a check today."

    22.____

C. "What is the worst that can happen to you if you don't pay for your child care this very day?"
D. "It would be against the law for me to do that."

23. Which of the following types of workers is MOST likely to be covered by a compulsory workers' compensation system? 23.____

    A. office assistant
    B. musician
    C. farm worker
    D. teacher

Questions 24 and 25 refer to Table A, below:

Table B
Number of paid claims (1,000s)

Injury year	Indemnity claims	Medical-only claims	Total claims
1984	40.2	103.2	143.4
1985	39.1	102.8	141.8
1988	37.8	101.2	138.7
1987	39.2	103.4	142.5
1988	42.0	109.9	151.9
1989	42.5	113.2	155.6
1990	42.6	113.3	155.8
1991	42.0	111.2	153.2
1992	39.4	112.8	152.2
1993	37.7	117.0	154.7
1994	37.1	125.4	162.5
1995	34.0	129.1	163.1
1996	33.8	131.4	165.2
1997	33.6	134.7	168.3
1998	32.8	134.4	167.2
1999	34.1	133.1	167.2
2000	34.7	132.5	167.1
2001	31.7	121.3	153.1
2002	29.4	109.1	138.6
2003	27.5	100.2	127.6
2004	26.5	97.4	124.0

24. The year in which the highest number of medical claims were filed was 24.____

    A. 1984
    B. 1990
    C. 1997
    D. 2000

25. The period during which total claims increased by the greatest number was 25.____

    A. 1987-1988
    B. 1991-1992
    C. 1993-1994
    D. 2001-2002

KEY (CORRECT ANSWERS)

1. B
2. C
3. A
4. C
5. B

6. D
7. B
8. D
9. C
10. C

11. A
12. A
13. B
14. A
15. B

16. B
17. C
18. D
19. A
20. D

21. D
22. A
23. A
24. C
25. A

TEST 3

DIRECTIONS: Each question or incomplete statement is followed by several suggested answers or completions. Select the one that BEST answers the question or completes the statement. *PRINT THE LETTER OF THE CORRECT ANSWER IN THE SPACE AT THE RIGHT.*

1. When the employer is classified by type, the _____ rating method is used to determine the premium rate.

    A. schedule
    B. manual
    C. retrospective
    D. experience

    1.____

2. Janet Smith, an employee of Yardbirds, Inc., suffers an accident on the job that has left her with a permanent partial disability. Before the accident, Janet worked 40 hours a week at a job that paid $10.00 an hour. After the accident, Janet returned to lighter-duty job that paid $8.00 an hour, again for a 40-hour week.

    Using a factor of 4.333 to arrive at a monthly figure, calculate Janet Smith's loss in earning capacity.

    A. $231.09 per month
    B. $346.64
    C. $887.96
    D. $1386.56

    2.____

3. Each of the following is a hazard associated with occupational disease, EXCEPT:

    A. sunlight
    B. noise
    C. exposure to toxic chemicals
    D. cigarette smoke

    3.____

4. _____ lost-wages benefits are paid to workers' compensation claimants for non-medical loss resulting from an injury or illness.

    A. Subrogation
    B. Capitalization
    C. Valuation
    D. Indemnity

    4.____

5. Common law requires that employers exercise reasonable care for the safety of their employees, including the specific duty to
    I. provide a safe work area and maintain the premises in safe condition
    II. warn employees of inherent dangers in the workplace, even those that are readily apparent
    III. provide enough competent employees for the work demanded
    IV. establish and enforce safety rules, in some cases to the point of discharging employees who repeatedly violate these rules

    5.____

A. I and II
B. I, II and III
C. II, III and IV
D. I, II, III and IV

6. Which of the following is NOT a type of rating plan that is typically used to calculate workers' compensation premiums?

    A. Experience rating
    B. Manual rating
    C. Assigned risk plans
    D. Premium discount plan

Questions 7 and 8 refer to the information below:

A state workers compensation program has a rehabilitative employment program that works as follows: a worker who works in an approved rehabilitative employment program will receive a standard total disability benefit (75 percent of average weekly wage) reduced by 50 percent of the income received for each week of rehabilitative employment.

Mike Spacely has worked for his company for six years, and his annual salary was $40,000 when he became disabled. He received total disability benefits for 14 weeks and then began work in an approved rehabilitative employment program. Because of his disability, Mike can only work 4 hours a day, and now earns $140 a week in rehabilitative employment.

7. During his 14 weeks of total disability, Mike earned a weekly benefit of approximately

    A. $507
    B. $578
    C. $647
    D. $769

8. During his rehabilitative employment, Mike earned a combined total of about _____, in both benefits and salary.

    A. $507
    B. $578
    C. $647
    D. $769

9. In a _____ for workers' compensation, the only variable affecting the premium that should change between the inception of the policy and an audit is payroll.

    A. retrospective rating
    B. guaranteed cost
    C. sliding scale dividend
    D. retention

10. The workers' compensation system was derived from the principle of vicarious liability, a tort doctrine that imposes responsibility upon one person for the failure of another. Another term for vicarious liability is _____ liability.

A. imputed
B. displaced
C. disputed
D. contributory

11. Under the standard workers compensation policy, the insurer agrees to make certain payments in addition to the statutory benefits. These additional payments typically include each of the following, EXCEPT

    A. litigation costs levied against the employer
    B. payments required due to failure to comply with health and safety regulations
    C. premiums for appeal bonds or bonds to release attachments
    D. interest accruing on a judgement until the insurer offers the amount due under the policy

12. The final step in compiling a disability rating is usually to

    A. adjust for the worker's occupational grouping
    B. adjust for diminished future earning capacity
    C. adjust for the worker's age on the date of injury
    D. apply the impairment standard

13. Which of the following is a medical test in which a medical practitioner uses an instrument to measure the range of motion in a joint?

    A. Joint calibration
    B. Flexion test
    C. Valsalva maneuver
    D. Goniometry

14. To protect some state and private insurers, a(n) _____ policy allows a reinsurer to reimburse a portion of a workers compensation claim with payments to the insurer after the insurer has made payments for a specified number of months of total disability.

    A. surplus-share
    B. quota-share
    C. excess-of-time
    D. excess-of-loss

15. Survivors who are entitled to compensation on a death claim generally include certain classes of dependents, including
    I. the surviving spouse
    II. surviving minor children, including adopted children
    III. a grandparent who was living with, and dependent on, the decedent
    IV. an uncle who was not described by the statute (i.e., lived apart from the decedent) but can prove his dependency on the decedent

    A. I only
    B. I and II
    C. I, II and III
    D. I, II, III and IV

4 (#3)

16. About two-thirds of U.S. state workers' compensation systems use rate-making standards established by the

   A. National Council on Compensation Insurance (NCCI)
   B. National Workers Compensation Defense Network (NWCDN)
   C. National Institute for Occupational Safety and Health (NIOSH)
   D. Federal Occupational Safety and Health Administration (OSHA)

16._____

17. Gerda has worked as a commissioned sales representative for Robo-cash since February 1 of 2005. On August 6 of 2007, she is injured on the job. Gerda's wages depend on her sales and are different every week. To calculate Gerda's weekly wage for the purpose of a workers' compensation claim, one should

   A. list all her weekly wages from 2/1/2005 to 11/6/2007. Then take the wage earned during the lowest-paying week, add it to the wage earned during the highest-paying week, and divide by two
   B. take Gerda's total earnings from 2/1/2005 to 11/6/2007 and divide by the total number of weeks she worked.
   C. list all her weekly wages from 2/1/2005 to 11/6/2007. Then find the median by dropping, alternately, each of the highest- or lowest-paying weeks until only one wage remains. If it is an even-numbered period of weeks, add the last two remaining wages and divide by one.
   D. consider only wages earned during the previous year, taking Gerda's total earnings from 11/6//2006 to 11/6/ 2007, and dividing by the total number of weeks she worked

17._____

18. A fully covered dependent of a disabled worker is eligible for 50% of federal disability benefits if the dependent is _____ of age or younger.

   A. 18
   B. 19
   C. 21
   D. 24

18._____

19. An employee who files a job-related stress claim must typically present a case in which work stress can be proven to have caused _____ percent of the psychiatric disability.

   A. 33
   B. 51
   C. 76
   D. 100

19._____

20. Workers' compensation claims generally fall into three categories. Which of the following is NOT one of them?

   A. Occupational disease
   B. Discrimination
   C. Injury
   D. Death

20._____

21. Most federal and state laws regarding workplace violence uphold the view that

21._____

43

A. employers' measures to prevent workplace violence should follow OSHA guidelines
B. employers are fail to prevent or abate a recognized violence hazard in the workplace may be held liable under the general duty clause
C. violence is unpredictable and therefore difficult, if not impossible, to prevent
D. unless the employer personally committed the violence, he or she cannot be held liable

22. What part of a workers compensation insurance contract is illustrated below? 22.____
(insurer) will pay for Total Disability or other covered loss resulting from Injuries or Sickness subject to the definitions, exclusions, and other provisions of this policy. Loss must begin while this policy is in force.

   A. benefit provision
   B. general provisions
   C. insuring clause
   D. payment of claims provision

23. Which of the following is a term for the degree to which certain factors may have caused or contributed to a particular impairment or disability? 23.____

   A. Assignation
   B. Degree of causation
   C. Aggravation
   D. Apportionment

24. An employee may have a legitimate discrimination claim against an employer if she files or plans to file a workers' compensation claim and is 24.____
   I. terminated from his or her job without good cause
   II. given a notice of controversion
   III. threatened with termination or other difficulties if she proceeds with the workers' compensation case
   IV. demoted or given a cut in pay without a reasonable business necessi

   A. I or II
   B. I, III or IV
   C. II and IV
   D. I, II, III and IV

25. If a worker is partially disabled, the benefit is typically payable as follows: 25.____

   $\dfrac{A-B}{A}$ x monthly benefit for total disability

   where:
   A = the worker's pre-claim monthly earnings
   B = the worker's monthly earnings for work in which partial disability is claimed

   Apply this formula to the following problem: John Doe had an annual salary of $66,000, and his employer's workers compensation insurance provided John a monthly total disability benefit of $3,500. After an on-the-job injury, John was able to return to work and earn $2,500 per month. His partial disability benefit would be

A. $546
B. $1,909
C. $2,154
D. $3500

KEY (CORRECT ANSWERS)

1.	D		11.	B
2.	B		12.	C
3.	D		13.	D
4.	D		14.	D
5.	D		15.	C
6.	C		16.	A
7.	B		17.	B
8.	C		18.	A
9.	B		19.	B
10.	A		20.	B

21. B
22. C
23. D
24. B
25. B

EXAMINATION SECTION
TEST 1

DIRECTIONS: Each question or incomplete statement is followed by several suggested answers or completions. Select the one that BEST answers the question or completes the statement. *PRINT THE LETTER OF THE CORRECT ANSWER IN THE SPACE AT THE RIGHT.*

1. A presumption of work-relatedness exists if a worker

   A. is unable to work because of the disease
   B. can provide an opinion from a physician that the disease is work-related
   C. caught the disease from a co-worker
   D. contracts a scheduled disease while working in the specified occupation

   1.____

2. Calculate the average weekly wage (AWW) of a ten-month (42-week) employee earning $30,000 annually.

   A. $576.92
   B. $714.29
   C. $989.56
   D. $1,260.00

   2.____

3. Cosmetic surgery is MOST likely to be covered under workers' compensation if it is

   A. elective
   B. performed by an agency-approved surgeon
   C. used to correct a pre-existing condition
   D. required as a result of a workplace accident

   3.____

4. The legal premise on which the workers' compensation system is based-workers give up the right to sue the employer in exchange for medical care of payment for their injuries-is known as

   A. conciliation
   B. sovereign immunity
   C. exclusive remedy
   D. covenants perpetual

   4.____

5. When talking with a claimant about a workers' compensation claim, open questioning would NOT generally be useful for

   A. determining the claimant's needs
   B. confirming the completeness of a claim
   C. getting more information about a case
   D. defining a problem

   5.____

6. The following passage is taken from the Workers' Compensation Provisions of the Consolidated Laws of New York State:

   (b) The first payment of compensation shall become due on the fourteenth day of disability on which date or within four days thereafter all compensation then due shall be paid, and the compensation payable bi-weekly thereafter; but the board may determine that any payments may be made monthly or at any other period, as it may deem advisable.

   6.____

Ralph, covered under the state system, is injured on the job on February 15th. Which of the following compensation dates would NOT conform with the statute?

- A. March 1
- B. March 7
- C. March 15
- D. March 28

7. Which of the following factors is NOT used to calculate partial disability indemnity?

    A. weekly or monthly indemnity amount
    B. premium
    C. loss of income
    D. prior income

8. Which of the following is NOT a common-law legal defense available to employers who, in states where workers' compensation is elective, need to defend themselves against industrial accidents?

    A. Assumption of risk
    B. Comparative negligence
    C. Contributory negligence
    D. Master-servant rule (fellow employee negligence)

9. Of the following cases, the employee LEAST likely be eligible for workers' compensation would be one who

    A. suffers panic attacks from hearing alarms or telephones ring loudly at work.
    B. suffers neck strain, blurred vision, and headaches from working long shifts at a computer monitor
    C. develops anxiety and panic attacks after witnessing a vicious assault and battery in the workplace
    D. fractures a hip when slipping on the ice and falling on the paved entrance to the employer's front door

10. An examiner is discussing a workers' compensation case with a claimant whose injuries have left her severely disabled. The most appropriate way to communicate with this client would be to

    A. watch for opportunities to offer assistance
    B. use language that focuses on her as a person, rather than her disability
    C. remember than disabled people are often uncomfortable or self-conscious when interacting with the nondisabled
    D. ignore the disability entirely

11. Which of the following statements is TRUE?

    A. While workers' compensation laws require employers to retain any punitive or exemplary damages assessed against them, employers' liability insurance provides coverage for punitive or exemplary damages.
    B. Under most workers' compensation statutes, employers still retain contributory negligence as a defense to workers' compensation claims.

C. The maximum benefit payable under workers compensation typically equals or exceeds 66.67 percent of the state's average wages.
D. An employer is not responsible, under the legal principle *respondeat superior,* for an injury caused solely by the negligence of fellow employee.

12. Common loss control techniques used in workers compensation include 12.____
    I. loss reduction
    II. avoidance
    III. loss prevention
    IV. contractual transfer

    A. I only
    B. I and III
    C. II, III and IV
    D. I, II, III and IV

When a job-related injury results in a permanent disability, an employee may be entitled to permanent partial disability (PPD) benefits based upon the degree of permanent disability. Often a body part or "scheduled member" is functionally impaired, leading an examiner or adjuster to consult a list of scheduled body members and their respective value, in number of weeks. Questions and are based on the list below:

Loss of thumb 60
Loss of first (index) finger 35
Loss of second finger 30
Loss of third finger 25
Loss of fourth finger 20
Loss of hand 190
Loss of arm 250
Loss of great toe 40
Loss of any other toe 15
Loss of foot 150
Loss of leg 220
Loss of eye 140
Loss of hearing in one ear 50
Loss of hearing in both ears 175
Permanent disfigurement, face or head 150

This schedule represents the number of weeks of benefits payable for 100% loss, or loss of use, of the body member. If the permanent partial disability rating is less than 100%, the percentage rating is multiplied by the number of weeks shown.

13. A claimant has suffered what a physician has described as a 20 percent loss in the use 13.____
    of his thumb. This claimant would receive_____
    weeks of PPD benefits.

    A. 6
    B. 12
    C. 48
    D. 60

14. A factory employee has lost entire leg-a 100 percent loss-in a workplace accident. His PPD benefits would be paid

    A. indefinitely, since it is a total disability.
    B. for 147 weeks
    C. for 220 weeks.
    D. none, since it qualifies as a principal-sum loss.

15. The experience modifier designates the first $5,000 of any single loss in a workers' compensation claim to be the _____ loss.

    A. instrumental
    B. primary
    C. intramarginal
    D. excess

16. Many states, such as New York, determine the compensation rate for temporary partial disability by calculating the average weekly wage, subtracting from that the current gross weekly wage being paid the injured employee, and multiplying that by two-thirds (.67). For example, if an employee were making $60(3 at an average weekly wage prior to the work injury and after the work injury was only making $400, the employee would be entitled to TPD benefits in the amount of_____ per week

    A. $66
    B. $134
    C. $268
    D. $333

17. _____ plans provide workers' compensation insurance to companies that do not meet the underwriting criteria of private insurers.

    A. Assigned risk
    B. Monopolistic
    C. Competitive
    D. Prorated

18. In most workers' compensation hearings, the degree of proof necessary for a claimant to prevail is

    A. beyond reasonable doubt
    B. clear and convincing evidence
    C. absolute proof
    D. preponderance of evidence

19. Lisa has missed work off and on for several months because of poor health. After a series of tests and visits, Laura's doctor tells her she has toxins in her system because of exposure to cleaning chemicals at work. In her state, Lisa has one year from the "date of injury" to file a workers' compensation claim. For this purpose, the "date of injury" would be the day

    A. Lisa missed her first day of work
    B. Lisa made her first visit to the doctor
    C. Lisa's doctor told her that her injuries were work-related
    D. Lisa informed her employer of the doctor"s diagnosis

20. John was temporarily disabled for about a year. On reviewing his records, John finds that during that time, he was not paid the full temporary disability benefit he was due; instead of receiving the full amount due, $336, he was paid $250. In the state where John works, a payment that has been unreasonably delayed or refused by an insurer is subject to a penalty of 25 percent or $10,000, whichever is less. John is due a total amount of

    A. $107.50
    B. $172
    C. $215
    D. $375

    20.____

21. Elliott, a corporate librarian, falls and injures his right knee at work. After his condition stabilizes, his doctor makes a finding of maximum medical improvement and gives him a "no heavy lifting" restriction. Elliott returns to his job at work, which does not involve heavy lifting. Typically, Elliott would

    A. be eligible for a permanent disability benefit, because her inability to lift heavy objects would limit her ability to find work on the open job market.
    B. not be eligible for either temporary or permanent disability benefits, since his job does not require heavy lifting.
    C. be reassigned to lighter duty and paid a permanent disability benefit.
    D. be eligible for a temporary disability benefit for the time he missed work, but no benefits thereafter, since his job doesn't involve heavy lifting.

    21.____

22. Workers' compensation insurance rates are typically affected by each of the following factors, EXCEPT the

    A. company's potential future losses
    B. number of employees in the company
    C. company's current profit or loss
    D. types of work performed at the company

    22.____

23. Which of the following terms is associated with third-party actions?

    A. Conveyance
    B. Subrogation
    C. Mediation
    D. Controversion

    23.____

24. _____ is a legal principle stating that if a person voluntarily assumes a risk and is injured as a result, she cannot be indemnified for the losses.

    A. Master-servant rule
    B. Caveat emptor
    C. Contributory negligence
    D. Assumption of risk

    24.____

25. While working for A-1 Cleaners, Mary inures her lower back on March 5, 2007. She files a workers' compensation claim and is treated by Dr. Jones, who treats her and sends her back to work with certain modifications and a 15 percent disability rating. Mary returns to work for A-I, and while still being treated for her previous injury, Mary suffers another back injury. She files another workers' compensation claim and is treated for that injury. Eventually Dr. Jones releases Mary back to work and writes a report stating that she reached maximum medical improvement on January 5, 2008 and has some permanent disability, caused half by the first injury and half by the second. The doctor gives Mary a restriction of "no heavy work."

    The permanent disability settlement for a 15 percent rating is $8,040 under state law. The permanent disability settlement for a 30 percent rating is $21,420. According to the facts above, Mary is entitled to

    A. no permanent disability benefits
    B. one settlement of $8,040
    C. two settlements of $8,040 each, for $ 16,080
    D. one settlement of $21,420

KEY (CORRECT ANSWERS)

1.	D	11.	C
2.	B	12.	D
3.	D	13.	B
4.	C	14.	C
5.	B	15.	B
6.	B	16.	B
7.	B	17.	A
8.	B	18.	D
9.	A	19.	C
10.	B	20.	C

21. A
22. C
23. B
24. D
25. D

TEST 2

DIRECTIONS: Each question or incomplete statement is followed by several suggested answers or completions. Select the one that BEST answers the question or completes the statement. *PRINT THE LETTER OF THE CORRECT ANSWER IN THE SPACE AT THE RIGHT.*

1. Most workers' compensation statutes generally require   1.____

    A. immediate payment of lost wages compensation, but a waiting period before medical care benefits are paid
    B. immediate payment of both lost wages and medical care benefits
    C. a waiting period before lost wages compensation are payable, but immediate payment of medical care benefits
    D. a waiting period before payment of both lost wages and benefits

2. Generally, the type of accident or injury that is LEAST likely to be in dispute as a basis for   2.____
   a workers' compensation claim is one that happens

    A. during company-sanctioned travel time
    B. off-site
    C. during the lunch or coffee break
    D. at the place of employment

3. The greatest cause of employee death is   3.____

    A. machinery-related accidents
    B. falls
    C. vehicular accidents
    D. occupational diseases

4. In researching a claim's history, an examiner comes across the term "permanent and   4.____
   stationary" in an older medical record. As of about 2005, the meaning of this term was
   changed to the concept of

    A. maximum medical improvement
    B. permanent partial disability
    C. permanent total disability
    D. supplemental job displacement benefits

5. Which of the following cases is NOT an example of neutral risk?   5.____

    A. a teacher injured in a drive-by shooting that occurs as she is at work in her classroom
    B. an automobile mechanic who is bitten by a dog while emptying used oil into an outdoor receptacle
    C. a window-washer injured in a fall from a scaffold
    D. an sales assistant struck by a falling tree as she walked to her car to embark on a call

6. Harriet, landscape gardener, injures her knees from constantly kneeling at work. Her doctor reports that she has attained maximum medical improvement on March 1, with a 15 percent permanent disability, payable at $230 a week. Her employer did not offer her any type of modified alternative work by May 1, so her payments increased by 15 percent. Her ongoing permanent disability benefit is

    A. $245
    B. $264.50
    C. $299
    D. $460

7. Minimal conditions must be met before financial responsibility can be assigned to a claim for workers' compensation. Which of the following is NOT one of them?

    A. A work-related accident or disability covered by workers' compensation law occurred.
    B. The employee or claimant notified the employer of the accident or disability within the required time limit.
    C. The employer is found to have at least some liability for the accident or disability.
    D. A causal relationship exists between the accident and a resulting injury or disability.

8. The purpose of a probationary period is to

    A. eliminate the need for a Medical Examiner's report
    B. protect the insurer against material misrepresentation
    C. protect the insurer company against preexisting conditions
    D. protect the worker against adverse selection

9. Often, state boards can overturn a workers' compensation award granted by an administrative law judge. In such cases, the ruling is said to have been
    I. annulled
    II. rescinded
    III. controverted
    IV. voided

    A. I or II
    B. I, II or IV
    C. II, III or IV
    D. I, II, III or IV

10. Jason, a long-haul truck driver who lives in Grass Valley, California, is hired at a Sacramento branch office of Cosmic Freight, Inc., a company headquartered in Reno, Nevada. In the course of his employment, Jason is injured in an accident in Oregon.

    Which of the following would typically be TRUE?

    A. Jason must receive benefits from the California state system.
    B. Jason may receive benefits from both the California and Nevada workers compensation systems, but not from Oregon.
    C. Jason may select the most generous benefits from the three systems, but may not receive duplicate benefits.
    D. Jason must file his claim in Oregon, where the accident occurred.

11. Typically, modified or alternative work offered by an employer must pay at least_____ percent of what the employee was paid at the time of his or her injury.

    A. 34
    B. 51
    C. 85
    D. 100

    11.____

12. The_____ benefit of some group insurance funds waives any premiums that fall due after the insured has been totally disabled for a specified period.

    A. total disability
    B. accelerated
    C. waiver of premium
    D. minimum participation

    12.____

13. Workers' compensation statutes generally cover most_____ employments, whether they are hazardous or not.
    I. public
    II. private
    III. domestic
    IV. agricultural

    A. I and II
    B. I, II and III
    C. II and III
    D. I, II, III and IV

    13.____

14. The time between the first day of disability and the day to which the disability must continue before it can result in the insured receiving benefits is known as the waiting or_____ period

    A. probationary
    B. eligibility
    C. elimination
    D. grace

    14.____

15. Which of the following is the term for a deviation from normal in a body part or organ system and its functioning?

    A. Impairment
    B. Physical restriction
    C. Disability
    D. Handicap

    15.____

16. Under federal OSHA regulations, all employers with_____ or more employees must maintain records of, and report, occupational injuries and occupational illnesses.

    A. 8
    B. 11
    C. 30
    D. 100

    16.____

17. Which of the following is a premium adjustment used for employers who are too small to qualify for an experience modifier?

    A. Merit rating
    B. Manual rating
    C. Attenuator
    D. Step-down

18. John Wilson works for Universal Construction, LLC. One day, while operating a backhoe, Wilson ruptured a water line, causing a flood that damaged several nearby buildings. While attempting to flee the rising waters, Wilson fractured his ankle. Most likely,

    A. Wilson is liable for the damages he caused, and is entitled to workers' compensation, if he is found to have deliberately ruptured the water line.
    B. Universal and Wilson will be jointly liable for damage to the building, but Wilson will be eligible for workers' compensation, whether he deliberately ruptured the water line or not.
    C. If he deliberately ruptured the water line, Wilson is liable for the damage he caused and is not entitled to workers' compensation.
    D. Whether Wilson meant to rupture the water line or not, his negligence in operating the backhoe will disqualify him from receiving workers' compensation.

19. Several U.S. states, along with Puerto Rico and the U.S. Virgin Islands, require all workers compensation insurance to be placed with the state or territorial fund. This approach is known as the_____. state fund

    A. competitive
    B. monopolistic
    C. autocratic
    D. assigned risk

20. In determining a disability rating, a rater will include the_____ _____, which is a whole-person impairment rating under the AMA Guides.

    A. impairment number
    B. impairment standard
    C. schedule amount
    D. impairment variant

21. On a telephone call with an employee who is awaiting a decision on an indexed claim, an examiner explains to the caller that even if he knew anything about the claim's progress through the process, he could not reveal anything about the progress of the claim. In order to best serve this customer, the examiner's response to him would be LEAST helpful if it involved

    A. explaining to the customer why no information is available yet
    B. quoting the passage in the state laws or regulations that prohibited this kind of communication
    C. make specific statements regarding what can be revealed about the claims process
    D. offering alternative solutions to the customer

22. Typically, a rated premium is based on dollars per $_____ of an employer's payroll. 22.____

    A. 10
    B. 100
    C. 1,000
    D. 10,000

23. Joe, who has worked for seven years at Geraldo's Auto Body, receives a substantial raise in July. In September, he slips on some grease on the shop floor and falls, fracturing his pelvis. In most jurisdiction's, Joe's average weekly wage will represent 23.____

    A. his average weekly earnings over the last 52 weeks
    B. his average weekly earnings up to July
    C. his weekly wage at the time of his injury
    D. the average between his current wage and the wage he was paid before his July raise

24. Pete, a firefighter, injures his back fighting a fire, and on August 15, his doctor submits a report of maximum medical improvement with a 15 percent disability rating, which is payable at $230 a week. On September 10, Pete's employer offers him an office job that will not require field work, and Paul accepts. His payments decrease by 15 percent, and his ongoing permanent disability payments are 24.____

    A. $0   24.____
    B. $195.50
    C. $245
    D. $264.50

25. If a worker is partially disabled, the benefit is typically payable as follows: 25.____

    $$\frac{A-B}{A} \times \text{weekly benefit for total disability A}$$

    where:
    A= the worker's pre-claim weekly earnings

    B= the worker's weekly earnings for work in which partial disability is claimed

    Apply this formula to the following problem: Stan Adams earns an average of $700 a week at Oil Changers, under a workers' compensation system that pays him a maximum weekly benefit of 75 percent of his average weekly wage. After slipping on some oil at work and wrenching his back, Stan is unable to change the oil in automobiles on the lift. His supervisor moves him to the position of greeter, where he writes down orders for incoming customers. The job pays only 80 percent of what Stan was earning as an oil changer, and he qualifies for partial disability.
    What is Stan's weekly partial disability benefit?

    A. $112
    B. $140
    C. $200
    D. $560

5 (#2)

KEY (CORRECT ANSWERS)

1.	C	11.	C
2.	D	12.	C
3.	C	13.	A
4.	A	14.	C
5.	C	15.	A
6.	B	16.	B
7.	C	17.	A
8.	C	18.	C
9.	B	19.	B
10.	C	20.	B

21. B
22. B
23. C
24. B
25. A

TEST 3

DIRECTIONS: Each question or incomplete statement is followed by several suggested answers or completions. Select the one that BEST answers the question or completes the statement. *PRINT THE LETTER OF THE CORRECT ANSWER IN THE SPACE AT THE RIGHT.*

1. A_____ fund is typically a state agency that reimburses self-insuring companies or insurance carriers for part of the workers' compensation costs in certain instances when an employee with a pre-existing permanent partial disability is injured on the job. 1.____

   A. group insurance
   B. retrospective
   C. second injury
   D. reinsurance

2. The two types of workers' compensation laws are 2.____

   A. statutory and administrative
   B. state-fund and self-insured
   C. criminal and civil
   D. compulsory and elective

3. The temporary total disability benefit is available to an employee when the employee is completely unable to work for a period of time. In a certain state, the TTD benefit is determined by multiplying the average weekly wage by two-thirds, or .67. As of the last regulatory revision, the maximum TTD benefit rate is $615.00. The minimum benefit rate is $104.00. 3.____

   Jack, who earns $600 a week, is injured on the job and is unable to work for a period of several weeks. His weekly benefit during that period would be

   A. 104
   B. 400
   C. 600
   D. 615

4. Each of the following is considered an accident prevention strategy, EXCEPT 4.____

   A. safety training and communications
   B. protective equipment
   C. selective hiring and firing
   D. work teams

5. Claims that are accepted by the employer or the insurer, but which may have unresolved issues, are typically sent by a state board or department to a process known as 5.____

   A. vetting
   B. conciliation
   C. arbitration
   D. controversion

6. For which of the following cases would the establishment of a valid workers' compensation claim be MOST difficult?

    A. A data-entry clerk who suffers tendonitis due to repetitive stress while telecommuting from his home computer
    B. A woman who slips and breaks her pelvis in the company lunchroom
    C. An office assistant who was attending an off-site business luncheon
    D. A traveling salesperson who is involved in an automobile accident while he is making his weekly rounds

7. Calculate the average weekly wage (AWW) of a 196-day employee earning $30,000.

    A. $576.92
    B. $714.29
    C. $765.30
    D. $1,071.43

8. The federal continual-training requirement states that employers must provide safety training for all new hires and those transferred into a department,

    A. even if only for one day
    B. if for a continuous period of five days
    C. if for a continuous period of 30 days
    D. when the transfer is meant to be permanent

9. The main reason an employer would protest a decision on a workers' compensation claim is because the employer feels that the claim

    A. does not adequately compensate the worker and his or her family
    B. results in a benefit that is greater than the claimant's base pay
    C. is fraudulent
    D. may effect its experience rating and result in a higher premium

10. The_____ doctrine states that employees who are injured on the job are entitled to workers' compensation benefits, but they cannot sue their employers for additional amounts.

    A. Feres
    B. quasi-contract
    C. generalized immunity
    D. exclusive remedy

11. Which of the following form titles would be filed by an insurance carrier or approved self-insurer?

    A. Application for Re-opening of Claim
    B. Notice that Right to Compensation is Controverted
    C. Application for Approval of Non-Schedule Adjustment
    D. Claim for Compensation and Notice of Commencement of Third Party Action

12. When a workers' compensation claim is caused by an occupational disease, most statutes establish a time limit for notifying one"s employer of either_____ from the date of disablement, or from the date when the claimant knew or should have known that the disease was due to the nature of the employment.

- A. 3 or 6 months
- B. 1 or 2 years
- C. 3 or 5 years
- D. 5 or 10 years

13. Workers' compensation insurers, whether state or private, play an important role in loss control. They often assist employers by offering
    I. financial incentives
    II. double indemnity protections
    III. risk management information services
    IV. accident prevention services

    - A. I, II and III
    - B. I, III and IV
    - C. II and IV
    - D. I, II, III and IV

14. A claimant has telephoned the examiner and appears to be mildly irritated to learn that all the required forms have not been submitted in order for his claim to be indexed. The most appropriate action for the examiner to take in order to attempt a resolution of this situation would be to

    - A. demonstrate a calm, emotional neutrality
    - B. allow the customer some time to vent her frustration
    - C. enlist the claimant's help in generating solutions
    - D. quietly but firmly suggest that the claimant calm down

15. When a workplace accident occurs, the employer can sustain a variety of losses that are not covered by its workers compensation or employers liability insurance. These uninsured losses typically include each of the following, EXCEPT costs or expenses that are

    - A. incurred by the insured at the insurer"s request
    - B. incurred because of missed deadlines or overtime expenses resulting from the loss of the employee
    - C. associated with damage to machines, tools, or other property affected by the accident
    - D. associated with hiring and training a new employee for the vacant position

16. In the state where Joshua works, employees are entitled to workers' compensation benefits up to two-thirds of their average weekly wage, within the minimum and maximum amounts allowed by law. Joshua is injured at work on February, 2007, and is assigned a 12 percent disability rating. The maximum average weekly amount allowed for an injury occurring in 2007 is $180 for a partial disability rating under 15 percent; $220 for a PD rating from 15 to 24.75 percent; $250 for a PD rating from 25 to 69.75 percent; and $280 for a PD rating of 70 percent or higher. Joshua, whose average weekly wage is $210 a week, is entitled to a maximum benefit amount of

    - A. $140
    - B. $180
    - C. $210
    - D. $220

17. The category of risk that is generally most problematic in determining the compensability of a work injury is _____ risk.

   A. directly employment-related
   B. neutral
   C. financial
   D. personal

18. Most disability rating schedules use _____ as the median age for adjusting a rating.

   A. 32
   B. 39
   C. 45
   D. 50

19. The partial disability benefit

   A. forces the worker to remain at home until he or she fully recovers.
   B. is payable for only a fraction of the policy's total disability benefit period.
   C. encourages injured employees to return to work.
   D. pays the insured for a presumptive disability.

20. The term for any single claim that exceeds $5,000 is classified by the experience modifier as a(n) _____ loss.

   A. excess
   B. proterm
   C. nonstandard
   D. rated

21. In California, no temporary disability benefits are paid for the first three days off work, unless the injury requires hospitalization or the employee misses more than 14 days of work. Frank is injured at work and takes 11 days off to recover. He was not hospitalized. He is entitled to _____ days of temporary disability.

   A. 3
   B. 8
   C. 11
   D. 14

22. An employee covered by workers' compensation is usually

   A. required to work with an insurer- or state-approved physician for workers' compensation puiposes, without condition
   B. required to work with an insurer- or state-approved physician for workers' compensation purposes, provided the insurer or state agency names the physician before an injury or accident occurs
   C. allowed to choose her treating physician for workers' compensation purposes, without condition
   D. allowed to choose her treating physician for workers' compensation purposes, provided the employer is notified of the employee's choice before the injury or accident occurs

23. The following passage is from the California Labor Code:

    3302. (a) (I) When a licensed contractor enters an agreement with a temporary employment agency, employment referral service, labor contractor, or other similar entity for the entity to supply the contractor with an individual to perform acts or contracts for which the contractor's license is required under Chapter 9 (commencing with Section 7000) of Division 3 of the Business and Professions Code and the licensed contractor is responsible for supervising the employee's work, the temporary employment agency, employment referral service, labor contractor, or other similar entity shall pay workers' compensation premiums based on the contractor's experience modification rating.

    Julius Jones, an office worker, is a client of People Power, Inc., a temporary employment agency. ABC Corporation, a large construction contractor, is hiring clerical staff for a large upcoming project in the downtown area: a new federal government office building complex. ABC hires Julius Jones, as a client of People Power, to perform clerical duties during the project.

    According to the section of the Labor Code above, the premiums for Julius Jones's workers' compensation insurance are to be paid by

    A. Julius Jones
    B. ABC Corporation
    C. People Power, Inc.
    D. the federal government

24. Although workers' compensation is established as a "no-fault" system, this has proven to be no longer true, in certain cases, for _____ injuries.

    A. continuous trauma
    B. psychiatric
    C. disfiguring
    D. respiratory

25.

Table D
Types of Injury in which at least 10 Percent of Claims Reach Statutory MMI

Body Part Injured	MMI Prior to 104 Weeks		MMI at 104 Weeks or More	
	Number of Claims	Percent of Claims	Number of Claims	Percent of Claims
Head (unspecified)	95	85.6%	16	14.4%
Brain	200	88.1%	27	11.9%
Circulatory System	104	86.7%	16	13.3%
Muscle-skeletal System	175	89.7%	20	10.3%
Nervous System	346	85.0%	61	15.0%
Respiratory System	131	85.1%	23	14.9%
Nature of injury				
Concussion	199	88.0%	27	12.0%
Cerebrovascular	56	83.6%	11	16.4%
Mental Disease	134	80.7%	32	19.3%
Ill-Defined Conditions	393	86.4%	62	13.6%

Based on the data in Table D above, what type of injury or illness is most likely to result in a finding of maximum medical improvement after 104 weeks have passed?
A. Mental disease
B. Brain or Concussion
C. Musculo-skeletal
D. Ill-defined conditions

KEY (CORRECT ANSWERS)

1. C
2. D
3. B
4. C
5. B

6. C
7. D
8. A
9. D
10. D

11. B
12. B
13. B
14. C
15. A

16. A
17. B
18. B
19. B
20. A

21. B
22. D
23. C
24. B
25. A

EXAMINATION SECTION
TEST 1

DIRECTIONS: Each question or incomplete statement is followed by several suggested answers or completions. Select the one that BEST answers the question or completes the statement. *PRINT THE LETTER OF THE CORRECT ANSWER IN THE SPACE AT THE RIGHT.*

Questions 1-15.

DIRECTIONS: In the following questions numbered 1 through 15, the word in capitals is the name of an anatomical part which is a segment of a larger structure or system For each question, select the letter preceding the structure or system of which the word in capitals is a part.

1. ESOPHAGUS

    A. circulatory system
    C. submaxillary
    B. bronchi
    D. respiratory system

2. ALVEOLI

    A. nervous system
    C. endocrine system
    B. lungs
    D. muscle

3. DELTOID

    A. upper arm
    C. circulatory system
    B. rib cage
    D. superior vena cava

4. FEMORAL ARTERY

    A. right ventricle
    C. circulatory system
    B. left auricle
    D. lymphatic system

5. BRACKIAL PLEXUS

    A. circulatory system
    C. respiratory system
    B. nervous system
    D. bronchi

6. ERYTHROCYTE

    A. lymph glands
    C. blood
    B. skeletal system
    D. large intestine

7. STERNUM

    A. spinal column
    C. nervous system
    B. muscular system
    D. skeletal system

8. THYMUS

    A. endocrine system
    C. parathyroids
    B. pituitary gland
    D. adrenals

9. MANDIBLE

    A. pelvis   B. head   C. liver   D. stomach

2 (#1)

10. PECTORAL

A. skeletal system B. patella
C. chest D. digestive tract

10.____

11. CORNEA

A. arm B. eye C. blood D. lymph

11.____

12. CRANIUM

A. circulatory system B. left auricle
C. skeletal system D. abdomen

12.____

13. TRAPEZIUS

A. breastbone B. muscular system
C. endocrine system D. spinal column

13.____

14. MEGALOBLAST

A. blood B. pelvis C. spleen D. head

14.____

15. ADRENAL

A. mouth B. respiratory system
C. liver D. endocrine system

15.____

Questions 16-25.

DIRECTIONS: The following questions numbered 16 through 25 are concerned with various categories of diseases. For each question, select the letter preceding the disease or condition which MOST properly belongs to the category listed.

16. BONE DISEASE

A. arrhythmia B. arthritis
C. edema D. gastritis

16.____

17. DISEASE OF THE DIGESTIVE SYSTEM

A. diabetes B. osteomyelitis
C. ileitis D. conjunctivitis

17.____

18. DISEASE OF THE RESPIRATORY SYSTEM

A. cyanosis B. poliomyelitis
C. jaundice D. bronchiectasis

18.____

19. DISEASE OF THE HEART

A. hepatitis B. influenza
C. encephalitis D. myocarditis

19.____

20. DISEASE OF THE BLOOD

A. leukemia B. diphtheria
C. pneumonia D. colitis

20.____

21. NUTRITIONAL DISEASE							21.____

    A. hyperemia						B. mononucleosis
    C. trichinosis						D. scurvy

22. DISEASE OF THE NERVOUS SYSTEM					22.____

    A. amebiasis						B. parkinsonism
    C. ascariasis						D. tapeworm

23. PARASITIC DISEASE							23.____

    A. salmonella						B. neuralgia
    C. hemophilia						D. bursitis

24. SKIN DISEASE							24.____

    A. hydrocephalus					B. leprosy
    C. adenitis						D. angina

25. DISEASE OF THE URINARY TRACT					25.____

    A. myasthenia gravis					B. colitis
    C. hydronephrosis					D. dermatitis

KEY (CORRECT ANSWERS)

1. D   11. B
2. B   12. C
3. A   13. B
4. C   14. A
5. B   15. D

6. C   16. B
7. D   17. C
8. A   18. D
9. B   19. D
10. C   20. A

21. D
22. B
23. A
24. B
25. C

TEST 2

DIRECTIONS: Each question or incomplete statement is followed by several suggested answers or completions. Select the one that BEST answers the question or completes the statement. *PRINT THE LETTER OF THE CORRECT ANSWER IN THE SPACE AT THE RIGHT.*

Questions 1-10.

DIRECTIONS: Questions 1 through 10 are concerned with various categories of diseases. For each question, select the letter preceding the disease or condition which MOST properly belongs to the category listed.

1. DISEASE OF THE HEART

    A. diabetes   B. tachycardia
    C. osteoporosis   D. adenitis

2. SKIN DISEASE

    A. cholelithiasis   B. colitis
    C. psoriasis   D. encephalitis

3. DISEASE OF THE BLOOD

    A. polycythemia   B. ileitis
    C. psoitis   D. dermatitis

4. DISEASE OF THE RESPIRATORY SYSTEM

    A. dysentery   B. angina
    C. hemophilia   D. pneumonia

5. DISEASE OF THE DIGESTIVE SYSTEM

    A. periastitis   B. bronchiectasis
    C. enteritis   D. pertussis

6. PARASITIC DISEASE

    A. ascariasis   B. nephritis
    C. hyperemia   D. neuralgia

7. NUTRITIONAL DISEASE

    A. entasis   B. pellagra
    C. amebiasis   D. diphtheria

8. BONE DISEASE

    A. gangrene   B. epilepsy
    C. osteochondritis   D. bronchitis

9. DISEASE OF THE NERVOUS SYSTEM

    A. mononucleosis   B. gallstones
    C. jaundice   D. multiple sclerosis

10. DISEASE OF THE URINARY TRACT 10.____

    A. hydrocephalus   B. glomerulonephritis
    C. cyanosis   D. bursitis

Questions 11-25.

DIRECTIONS: For the following questions 11 through 25, select the letter preceding the part or system of the body which is CHIEFLY affected by the disease in capitals.

11. CONJUNCTIVITIS 11.____

    A. ear   B. intestines
    C. eye   D. liver

12. EMPHYSEMA 12.____

    A. heart   B. bronchial tubes
    C. pancreas   D. lymph nodes

13. CHOLELITHIASIS 13.____

    A. muscles   B. liver
    C. bones   D. common bile duct

14. PYELONEPHRITIS 14.____

    A. intestinal tract   B. arterial walls
    C. ligaments   D. urinary tract

15. EPILEPSY 15.____

    A. nervous system   B. pancreas
    C. thyroid   D. stomach

16. DYSENTERY 16.____

    A. tendons   B. kidneys
    C. intestines   D. brain

17. ERYTHROBLASTOSIS 17.____

    A. kidneys   B. blood
    C. endocrine system   D. large intestine

18. GLAUCOMA 18.____

    A. blood vessels   B. cortex
    C. cerebellum   D. eye

19. OSTEOPOROSIS 19.____

    A. bones   B. central nervous system
    C. adrenals   D. lymph nodes

20. MENINGITIS 20.____

    A. nasal passages   B. intestinal tract
    C. spinal cord   D. urinary tract

21. BURSITIS   21._____
    A. urinary tract   B. bones
    C. nasal passages   D. heart

22. ENDOCARDITIS   22._____
    A. cortex   B. kidneys   C. pancreas   D. heart

23. DIVERTICULOSIS   23._____
    A. thyroid   B. endocrine system
    C. intestinal tract   D. kidneys

24. ENCEPHALITIS   24._____
    A. brain   B. vessels   C. kidneys   D. eye

25. ILEITIS   25._____
    A. nervous system   B. blood
    C. liver   D. intestinal tract

KEY (CORRECT ANSWERS)

1.	B	11.	C
2.	C	12.	B
3.	A	13.	D
4.	D	14.	D
5.	C	15.	A
6.	A	16.	C
7.	B	17.	B
8.	C	18.	D
9.	D	19.	A
10.	B	20.	C

21. B
22. D
23. C
24. A
25. D

EXAMINATION SECTION
TEST 1

DIRECTIONS: Each question or incomplete statement is followed by several suggested answers or completions. Select the one that BEST answers the question or completes the statement. *PRINT THE LETTER OF THE CORRECT ANSWER IN THE SPACE AT THE RIGHT.*

Questions 1-20.

DIRECTIONS: Column I below lists words used in medical practice. Column II lists phrases which describe the words in Column I. Opposite the number preceding each of the words in Column I, place the letter preceding the phrase in Column II which BEST describes the word in Column I.

COLUMN I

1. Abrasion
2. Aseptic
3. Cardiac
4. Catarrh
5. Contamination
6. Dermatology
7. Disinfectant
8. Dyspepsia
9. Epidemic
10. Epidermis
11. Incubation
12. Microscope
13. Pediatrics
14. Plasma
15. Prenatal
16. Retina
17. Syphilis
18. Syringe
19. Toxemia
20. Vaccine

COLUMN II

A. A disturbance of digestion
B. Destroying the germs of disease
C. A general poisoning of the blood
D. An instrument used for injecting fluids
E. A scraping off of the skin
F. Free from disease germs
G. An apparatus for viewing internal organs by means of x-rays
H. An instrument for assisting the eye in observing minute objects
I. An inoculable immunizing agent
J. The extensive prevalence in a community of a
K. Chemical product of an organ
L. Preceding birth
M. Fever
N. The branch of medical science that relates to the skin and its diseases
O. Fluid part of the blood
P. The science of the hygienic care of children
Q. Infection by contact
R. Relating to the heart
S. Inner structure of the eye
T. Outer portion of the skin
U. Pertaining to the ductless glands
V. An infectious venereal disease
W. The development of an infectious disease from the period of infection to that of the appearance of the first symptoms
X. Simple inflammation of a mucous membrane
Y. An instrument for measuring blood pressure

1.____
2.____
3.____
4.____
5.____
6.____
7.____
8.____
9.____
10.____
11.____
12.____
13.____
14.____
15.____
16.____
17.____
18.____
19.____
20.____

Questions 21-25.

DIRECTIONS: Each of Questions 21 through 25 consists of four words. Three of these words belong together. One word does NOT belong with the other three. For each group of words, you are to select the one word which does NOT belong with the other three words.

21. A. conclude   B. terminate   C. initiate   D. end   21.___

22. A. deficient   B. inadequate   22.___
    C. excessive   D. insufficient

23. A. rare   B. unique   C. unusual   D. frequent   23.___

24. A. unquestionable   B. uncertain   24.___
    C. doubtful   D. indefinite

25. A. stretch   B. contract   C. extend   D. expand   25.___

KEY (CORRECT ANSWERS)

1. E
2. F
3. R
4. X
5. Q
6. N
7. B
8. A
9. J
10. T

11. W
12. H
13. P
14. O
15. L
16. S
17. V
18. D
19. C
20. I

21. C
22. C
23. D
24. A
25. B

TEST 2

DIRECTIONS: Each question or incomplete statement is followed by several suggested answers or completions. Select the one that BEST answers the question or completes the statement. *PRINT THE LETTER OF THE CORRECT ANSWER IN THE SPACE AT THE RIGHT.*

Questions 1-4.

DIRECTIONS: Questions 1 through 4 pertain to the meaning of terms which may be encountered in laboratory work. For each question, select the option whose meaning is MOST NEARLY the same as that of the numbered item.

1. Atrophied
   - A. enlarged
   - B. relaxed
   - C. strengthened
   - D. wasted

2. Leucocyte
   - A. white cell
   - B. red cell
   - C. epithelial cell
   - D. dermal cell

3. Permeable
   - A. volatile
   - B. variable
   - C. flexible
   - D. penetrable

4. Attenuate
   - A. dilute
   - B. infect
   - C. oxidize
   - D. strengthen

Questions 5-11.

DIRECTIONS: For Questions 5 through 11, select the letter preceding the word which means MOST NEARLY the same as the first word.

5. legible
   - A. readable
   - B. eligible
   - C. learned
   - D. lawful

6. observe
   - A. assist
   - B. watch
   - C. correct
   - D. oppose

7. habitual
   - A. punctual
   - B. occasional
   - C. usual
   - D. actual

8. chronological
   - A. successive
   - B. earlier
   - C. later
   - D. studious

9. arrest

   A. punish   B. run   C. threaten   D. stop

10. abstain

    A. refrain   B. indulge   C. discolor   D. spoil

11. toxic

    A. poisonous   B. decaying
    C. taxing   D. defective

12. The *initial* contact is of great importance in setting a pattern for future relations.
    The word *initial*, as used in this sentence, means MOST NEARLY

    A. first   B. written   C. direct   D. hidden

13. The doctor prescribed a diet which was *adequate* for the patient's needs.
    The word *adequate*, as used in this sentence, means MOST NEARLY

    A. insufficient   B. unusual
    C. required   D. enough

14. The child was reported to be suffering from a vitamin *deficiency*.
    The word *deficiency*, as used in this sentence, means MOST NEARLY

    A. surplus   B. infection   C. shortage   D. injury

15. In obtaining medical case data, a medical record librarian should discourage the patient from giving *irrelevant* information.
    The word *irrelevant*, as used in this sentence, means MOST NEARLY

    A. too detailed   B. pertaining to relatives
    C. insufficient   D. inappropriate

16. The doctor requested that a *tentative* appointment be made for the patient.
    The word *tentative*, as used in this sentence, means MOST NEARLY

    A. definite   B. subject to change
    C. later   D. of short duration

17. The black plague resulted in an usually high *mortality rate* in the population of Europe.
    The term *mortality rate*, as used in this sentence, means MOST NEARLY

    A. future immunity of the people
    B. death rate
    C. general weakening of the health of the people
    D. sickness rate

18. The public health assistant was asked to file a number of *identical* reports on the case.
    The word *identical*, as used in this sentence, means MOST NEARLY

    A. accurate   B. detailed   C. same   D. different

19. The nurse assisted in *the biopsy* of the patient.
    The word *biopsy*, as used in this sentence, means MOST NEARLY

    A. autopsy
    B. excision and diagnostic study of tissue
    C. biography and health history
    D. administering of anesthesia

20. The assistant noted that the swelling on the patient's face had *subsided*.
    The word *subsided*, as used in this sentence, means MOST NEARLY

    A. become aggravated   B. increased
    C. vanished   D. abated

21. The patient was given food *intravenously*.
    The word *intravenously*, as used in this sentence, means MOST NEARLY

    A. orally   B. against his will
    C. through the veins   D. without condiment

Questions 22-25.

DIRECTIONS: Each of Questions 22 through 25 consists of four words. Three of these words belong together. One word does NOT belong with the other three. For each group of words, you are to select the one word which does NOT belong with the other three words.

22. A. accelerate   B. quicken   C. accept   D. hasten
23. A. sever   B. rupture   C. rectify   D. tear
24. A. innocuous   B. injurious C. dangerous   D. harmful
25. A. adulterate   B. contaminate
     C. taint   D. disinfect

KEY (CORRECT ANSWERS)

1. D	11. A	21. C
2. A	12. A	22. C
3. D	13. D	23. C
4. A	14. C	24. A
5. A	15. D	25. D
6. B	16. B	
7. C	17. B	
8. A	18. C	
9. D	19. B	
10. A	20. D	

TEST 3

DIRECTIONS: Each question or incomplete statement is followed by several suggested answers or completions. Select the one that BEST answers the question or completes the statement. *PRINT THE LETTER OF THE CORRECT ANSWER IN THE SPACE AT THE RIGHT.*

Questions 1-25.

DIRECTIONS: Each of Questions 1 through 25 consists of a word, in capitals, followed by four suggested meanings of the word. For each question, indicate in the space at the right the letter preceding the word which means MOST NEARLY the same as the word in capitals.

1. TEMPORARY
   - A. permanently
   - B. for a limited time
   - C. at the same time
   - D. frequently

   1.____

2. INQUIRE
   - A. order
   - B. agree
   - C. ask
   - D. discharge

   2.____

3. SUFFICIENT
   - A. enough
   - B. inadequate
   - C. thorough
   - D. capable

   3.____

4. AMBULATORY
   - A. bedridden
   - B. left-handed
   - C. walking
   - D. laboratory

   4.____

5. DILATE
   - A. enlarge
   - B. contract
   - C. revise
   - D. restrict

   5.____

6. NUTRITIOUS
   - A. protective
   - B. healthful
   - C. fattening
   - D. nourishing

   6.____

7. CONGENITAL
   - A. with pleasure
   - B. defective
   - C. likeable
   - D. existing from birth

   7.____

8. ISOLATION
   - A. sanitation
   - B. quarantine
   - C. rudeness
   - D. exposure

   8.____

9. SPASM
   - A. splash
   - B. twitch
   - C. space
   - D. blow

   9.____

10. HEMORRHAGE   10.____
    A. bleeding   B. ulcer
    C. hereditary disease   D. lack of blood

11. NOXIOUS   11.____
    A. gaseous   B. harmful   C. soothing   D. repulsive

12. PYOGENIC   12.____
    A. disease producing   B. fever producing
    C. pus forming   D. water forming

13. RENAL   13.____
    A. brain   B. heart   C. kidney   D. stomach

14. ENDEMIC   14.____
    A. epidemic
    B. endermic
    C. endoblast
    D. peculiar to a particular people or locality, as a disease

15. MACULATION   15.____
    A. reticulation   B. inoculation
    C. maturation   D. defilement

16. TOLERATE   16.____
    A. fear   B. forgive   C. allow   D. despise

17. VENTILATE   17.____
    A. vacate   B. air   C. extricate   D. heat

18. SUPERIOR   18.____
    A. perfect   B. subordinate
    C. lower   D. higher

19. EXTREMITY   19.____
    A. extent   B. limb   C. illness   D. execution

20. DIVULGED   20.____
    A. unrefined   B. secreted   C. revealed   D. divided

21. SIPHON   21.____
    A. drain   B. drink   C. compute   D. discard

22. EXPIRATION   22.____
    A. trip   B. demonstration
    C. examination   D. end

23. AEROSOL
   A. a gas dispersed in a liquid
   B. a liquid dispersed in a gas
   C. a liquid dispersed in a solid
   D. a solid dispersed in a liquid

24. ETIOLOGY
   A. cause of a disease
   B. method of cure
   C. method of diagnosis
   D. study of insects

25. IN VITRO
   A. in alkali
   B. in the body
   C. in the test tube
   D. in vacuum

KEY (CORRECT ANSWERS)

1.	B		11.	B
2.	C		12.	C
3.	A		13.	C
4.	C		14.	D
5.	A		15.	D
6.	D		16.	C
7.	D		17.	B
8.	B		18.	D
9.	B		19.	B
10.	A		20.	C

21. A
22. D
23. B
24. A
25. C

READING COMPREHENSION
UNDERSTANDING AND INTERPRETING WRITTEN MATERIAL
EXAMINATION SECTION
TEST 1

Questions 1-8.

DIRECTIONS: Each question or incomplete statement is followed by several suggested answers or completions. Select the one that BEST answers the question or completes the statement. *PRINT THE LETTER OF THE CORRECT ANSWER IN THE SPACE AT THE RIGHT.*

Questions 1 and 2.

DIRECTIONS: Your answers to Questions 1 and 2 must be based ONLY on the information given in the following paragraph.

Hospitals maintained wholly by public taxation may treat only those compensation cases which are emergencies and may not treat such emergency cases longer than the emergency exists; provided, however, that these restrictions shall not be applicable where there is not available a hospital other than a hospital maintained wholly by taxation.

1. According to the above paragraph, compensation cases

    A. are regarded as emergency cases by hospitals maintained wholly by public taxation
    B. are seldom treated by hospitals maintained wholly by public taxation
    C. are treated mainly by privately endowed hospitals
    D. may be treated by hospitals maintained wholly by public taxation if they are emergencies

2. According to the above paragraph, it is MOST reasonable to conclude that where a privately endowed hospital is available,

    A. a hospital supported wholly by public taxation may treat emergency compensation cases only so long as the emergency exists
    B. a hospital supported wholly by public taxation may treat any compensation cases
    C. a hospital supported wholly by public taxation must refer emergency compensation cases to such a hospital
    D. the restrictions regarding the treatment of compensation cases by a tax-supported hospital are not wholly applicable

Questions 3-7.

DIRECTIONS: Answer Questions 3 through 7 ONLY according to the information given in the following passage.

THE MANUFACTURE OF LAUNDRY SOAP

The manufacture of soap is not a complicated process. Soap is a fat or an oil, plus an alkali, water and salt. The alkali used in making commercial laundry soap is caustic soda. The salt used is the same as common table salt. A fat is generally an animal product that is not a liquid at room temperature. If heated, it becomes a liquid. An oil is generally liquid at room temperature. If the temperature is lowered, the oil becomes a solid just like ordinary fat.

At the soap plant, a huge tank five stories high, called a *kettle,* is first filled part way with fats and then the alkali and water are added. These ingredients are then heated and boiled together. Salt is then poured into the top of the boiling solution; and as the salt slowly sinks down through the mixture, it takes with it the glycerine which comes from the melted fats. The product which finally comes from the kettle is a clear soap which has a moisture content of about 34%. This clear soap is then chilled so that more moisture is driven out. As a result, the manufacturer finally ends up with a commercial laundry soap consisting of 88% clear soap and only 12% moisture.

3. An ingredient used in making laundry soap is

   A. table sugar B. potash
   C. glycerine   D. caustic soda

4. According to the above passage, a difference between fats and oils is that fats

   A. cost more than oils
   B. are solid at room temperature
   C. have less water than oils
   D. are a liquid animal product

5. According to the above passage, the MAIN reason for using salt in the manufacture of soap is to

   A. make the ingredients boil together
   B. keep the fats in the kettle melted
   C. remove the glycerine
   D. prevent the loss of water from the soap

6. According to the passage, the purpose of chilling the clear soap is to

   A. stop the glycerine from melting
   B. separate the alkali from the fats
   C. make the oil become solid
   D. get rid of more moisture

7. According to the passage, the percentage of moisture in commercial laundry soap is

   A. 12%   B. 34%   C. 66%   D. 88%

8. The x-ray has gone into business. Developed primarily to aid in diagnosing human ills, the machine now works in packing plants, in foundries, in service stations, and in a dozen ways to contribute to precision and accuracy in industry.
   The above statement means *most nearly* that the x-ray

   A. was first developed to aid business
   B. is of more help to business than it is to medicine
   C. is being used to improve the functioning of business
   D. is more accurate for packing plants than it is for foundries

8.____

Questions 9-25.

DIRECTIONS: Each question consists of a statement. You are to indicate whether the statement is TRUE (T) or FALSE (F). *PRINT THE LETTER OF THE CORRECT ANSWER IN THE SPACE AT THE RIGHT.*

Questions 9-12.

DIRECTIONS: Read the paragraph below about *shock* and then answer Questions 9 through 12 according to the information given in the paragraph.

SHOCK

While not found in all injuries, shock is present in all serious injuries caused by accidents. During shock, the normal activities of the body slow down. This partly explains why one of the signs of shock is a pale, cold skin, since insufficient blood goes to the body parts during shock.

9. If the injury caused by an accident is serious, shock is sure to be present. 9.____

10. In shock, the heart beats faster than normal. 10.____

11. The face of a person suffering from shock is usually red and flushed. 11.____

12. Not enough blood goes to different parts of the body during shock. 12.____

Questions 13-18.

DIRECTIONS: Questions 13 through 18, inclusive, are to be answered SOLELY on the basis of the information contained in the following statement and NOT upon any other information you may have.

Blood transfusions are given to patients at the hospital upon recommendation of the physicians attending such cases. The physician fills out a *Request for Blood Transfusion* form in duplicate and sends both copies to the Medical Director's office, where a list is maintained of persons called *donors* who desire to sell their blood for transfusions. A suitable donor is selected, and the transfusion is given. Donors are, in many instances, medical students and employees of the hospital. Donors receive twenty-five dollars for each transfusion.

13. According to the above paragraph, a blood donor is paid twenty-five dollars for each transfusion. 13.____

14. According to the above paragraph, only medical students and employees of the hospital are selected as blood donors. 14.___

15. According to the above paragraph, the *Request for Blood Transfusion* form is filled out by the patient and sent to the Medical Director's office. 15.___

16. According to the above paragraph, a list of blood donors is maintained in the Medical Director's office. 16.___

17. According to the above paragraph, cases for which the attending physicians recommend blood transfusions are usually emergency cases. 17.___

18. According to the above paragraph, one copy of the *Request for Blood Transfusion* form is kept by the patient and one copy is sent to the Medical Director's office. 18.___

Questions 19-25.

DIRECTIONS: Questions 19 through 25, inclusive, are to be answered SOLELY on the basis of the information contained in the following passage and NOT upon any other information you may have.

Before being admitted to a hospital ward, a patient is first interviewed by the Admitting Clerk, who records the patient's name, age, sex, race, birthplace, and mother's maiden name. This clerk takes all of the money and valuables that the patient has on his person. A list of the valuables is written on the back of the envelope in which the valuables are afterwards placed. Cash is counted and placed in a separate envelope, and the amount of money and the name of the patient are written on the outside of the envelope. Both envelopes are sealed, fastened together, and placed in a compartment of a safe.

An orderly then escorts the patient to a dressing room where the patient's clothes are removed and placed in a bundle. A tag bearing the patient's name is fastened to the bundle. A list of the contents of the bundle is written on property slips, which are made out in triplicate. The information contained on the outside of the envelopes containing the cash and valuables belonging to the patient is also copied on the property slips.

According to the above passage,

19. patients are escorted to the dressing room by the Admitting Clerk. 19.___

20. the patient's cash and valuables are placed together in one envelope. 20.___

21. the number of identical property slips that are made out when a patient is being admitted to a hospital ward is three. 21.___

22. the full names of both parents of a patient are recorded by the Admitting Clerk before a patient is admitted to a hospital ward. 22.___

23. the amount of money that a patient has on his person when admitted to the hospital is entered on the patient's property slips. 23.___

24. an orderly takes all the money and valuables that a patient has on his person. 24.___

25. the patient's name is placed on the tag that is attached to the bundle containing the patient's clothing. 25.___

KEY (CORRECT ANSWERS)

1. D
2. A
3. D
4. B
5. C

6. D
7. A
8. C
9. T
10. F

11. F
12. T
13. T
14. F
15. F

16. T
17. T
18. F
19. F
20. F

21. T
22. F
23. T
24. F
25. T

TEST 2

DIRECTIONS: Each question or incomplete statement is followed by several suggested answers or completions. Select the one that BEST answers the question or completes the statement. *PRINT THE LETTER OF THE CORRECT ANSWER IN THE SPACE AT THE RIGHT.*

Questions 1-4.

DIRECTIONS: Questions 1 through 4 are to be answered in accordance with the following paragraphs.

One fundamental difference between the United States health care system and the health care systems of some European countries is the way that hospital charges for long-term illnesses affect their citizens.

In European countries such as England, Sweden, and Germany, citizens can face, without fear, hospital charges due to prolonged illness, no matter how substantial they may be. Citizens of these nations are required to pay nothing when they are hospitalized, for they have prepaid their treatment as taxpayers when they were well and were earning incomes.

On the other hand, the United States citizen, in spite of the growth of payments by third parties which include private insurance carriers as well as public resources, has still to shoulder 40 percent of hospital care costs, while his private insurance contributes only 25 percent and public resources the remaining 35 percent.

Despite expansion of private health insurance and social legislation in the United States, out-of-pocket payments for hospital care by individuals have steadily increased. Such payments, currently totalling $23 billion, are nearly twice as high as ten years ago.

Reform is inevitable and, when it comes, will have to reconcile sharply conflicting interests. Hospital staffs are demanding higher and higher wages. Hospitals are under pressure by citizens, who as patients demand more and better services but who as taxpayers or as subscribers to hospital insurance plans, are reluctant to pay the higher cost of improved care. An acceptable reconciliation of these interests has so far eluded legislators and health administrators in the United States.

1. According to the above passage, the one of the following which is an ADVANTAGE that citizens of England, Sweden, and Germany have over United States citizens is that, when faced with long-term illness,

    A. the amount of out-of-pocket payments made by these European citizens is small when compared to out-of-pocket payments made by United States citizens
    B. European citizens have no fear of hospital costs no matter how great they may be
    C. more efficient and reliable hospitals are available to the European citizen than is available to the United States citizens
    D. a greater range of specialized hospital care is available to the European citizens than is available to the United States citizens

1.___

2. According to the above passage, reform of the United States system of health care must reconcile all of the following EXCEPT   2.____
   A. attempts by health administrators to provide improved hospital care
   B. taxpayers' reluctance to pay for the cost of more and better hospital services
   C. demands by hospital personnel for higher wages
   D. insurance subscribers' reluctance to pay the higher costs of improved hospital care

3. According to the above passage, the out-of-pocket payments for hospital care that individuals made ten years ago was APPROXIMATELY _____ billion.   3.____
   A. $32   B. $23   C. $12   D. $3

4. According to the above passage, the GREATEST share of the costs of hospital care in the United States is paid by   4.____
   A. United States citizens   B. private insurance carriers
   C. public resources   D. third parties

Questions 5-8.

DIRECTIONS: Questions 5 through 8 are to be answered SOLELY on the basis of the information contained in the following passage.

Effective cost controls have been difficult to establish in most hospitals in the United States. Ways must be found to operate hospitals with reasonable efficiency without sacrificing quality and in a manner that will reduce the amount of personal income now being spent on health care and the enormous drain on national resources. We must adopt a new public objective of providing higher quality health care at significantly lower cost. One step that can be taken to achieve this goal is to carefully control capital expenditures for hospital construction and expansion. Perhaps the way to start is to declare a moratorium on all hospital construction and to determine the factors that should be considered in deciding whether a hospital should be built. Such factors might include population growth, distance to the nearest hospital, availability of medical personnel, and hospital bed shortage.

A second step to achieve the new objective is to increase the ratio of out-of-hospital patient to in-hospital patient care. This can be done by using separate health care facilities other than hospitals to attract patients who have increasingly been going to hospital clinics and overcrowding them. Patients should instead identify with a separate health care facility to keep them out of hospitals.

A third step is to require better hospital operating rules and controls. This step might include the review of a doctor's performance by other doctors, outside professional evaluations of medical practice, and required refresher courses and re-examinations for doctors. Other measures might include obtaining mandatory second opinions on the need for surgery in order to avoid unnecessary surgery, and outside review of work rules and procedures to eliminate unnecessary testing of patients.

A fourth step is to halt the construction and public subsidizing of new medical schools and to fill whatever needs exist in professional coverage by emphasizing the medical training of physicians with specialities that are in short supply and by providing a better geographic distribution of physicians and surgeons.

5. According to the above passage, providing higher quality health care at lower cost can be achieved by the

   A. greater use of out-of-hospital facilities
   B. application of more effective cost controls on doctors' fees
   C. expansion of improved in-hospital patient care services at hospital clinics
   D. development of more effective training programs in hospital administration

6. According to the above passage, the one of the following which should be taken into account in determining if a hospital should be constructed is the

   A. number of out-of-hospital health care facilities
   B. availability of public funds to subsidize construction
   C. number of hospitals under construction
   D. availability of medical personnel

7. According to the above passage, it is IMPORTANT to operate hospitals efficiently because

   A. they are currently in serious financial difficulties
   B. of the need to reduce the amount of personal income going to health care
   C. the quality of health care services has deteriorated
   D. of the need to increase productivity goals to take care of the growing population in the United States

8. According to the above passage, which one of the following approaches is MOST LIKELY to result in better operating rules and controls in hospitals?

   A. Allocating doctors to health care facilities on the basis of patient population
   B. Equalizing the workloads of doctors
   C. Establishing a physician review board to evaluate the performance of other physicians
   D. Eliminating unnecessary outside review of patient testing

Questions 9-14.

DIRECTIONS: Questions 9 through 14 are to be answered SOLELY on the basis of the information contained in the following passage.

The United States today is the only major industrial nation in the world without a system of national health insurance or a national health service. Instead, we have placed our prime reliance on private enterprise and private health insurance to meet the need. Yet, in a recent year, of the 180 million Americans under 65 years of age, 34 million had no hospital insurance, 38 million had no surgical insurance, 63 million had no out-patient x-ray and laboratory insurance, 94 million had no insurance for prescription drugs, and 103 million had no insurance for physician office visits or home visits. Some 35 million Americans under the age of 65 had no health insurance whatsoever. Some 64 million additional Americans under age 65 had health insurance coverage that was less than that provided to the aged under Medicare.

Despite more than three decades of enormous growth, the private health insurance industry today pays benefits equal to only one-third of the total cost of private health care, leaving the rest to be borne by the patient—essentially the same ratio which held true a decade ago. Moreover, nearly all private health insurance is limited; it provides partial benefits, not comprehensive benefits; acute care, not preventive care; it siphons off the young and healthy, and ignores the poor and medically indigent. The typical private carrier usually pays only the cost of hospital care, forcing physicians and patients alike to resort to wasteful and inefficient use of hospital facilities, thereby giving further impetus to the already soaring costs of hospital care. Valuable hospital beds are used for routine tests and examinations. Unnecessary hospitalization, unnecessary surgery, and unnecessarily extended hospital stays are encouraged. These problems are exacerbated by the fact that administrative costs of commercial carriers are substantially higher than they are for Blue Shield, Blue Cross, or Medicare.

9. According to the above passage, the PROPORTION of total private health care costs paid by private health insurance companies today as compared to ten years ago has

   A. *increased* by approximately one-third
   B. *remained* practically the same
   C. *increased* by approximately two-thirds
   D. *decreased* by approximately one-third

10. According to the above passage, the one of the following which has contributed MOST to wasteful use of hospital facilities is the

    A. increased emphasis on preventive health care
    B. practice of private carriers of providing comprehensive health care benefits
    C. increased hospitalization of the elderly and the poor
    D. practice of a number of private carriers of paying only for hospital care costs

11. Based on the information in the above passage, which one of the following patients would be LEAST likely to receive benefits from a typical private health insurance plan?
    A

    A. young patient who must undergo an emergency appendectomy
    B. middle-aged patient who needs a costly series of x-ray and laboratory tests for diagnosis of gastrointestinal complaints
    C. young patient who must visit his physician weekly for treatment of a chronic skin disease
    D. middle-aged patient who requires extensive cancer surgery

12. Which one of the following is the MOST accurate inference that can be drawn from the above passage?

    A. Private health insurance has failed to fully meet the health care needs of Americans.
    B. Most Americans under age 65 have health insurance coverage better than that provided to the elderly under Medicare.
    C. Countries with a national health service are likely to provide poorer health care for their citizens than do countries that rely primarily on private health insurance.
    D. Hospital facilities in the United States are inadequate to meet the nation's health care needs.

13. Of the total number of Americans under age 65, what percentage belonged in the combined category of persons with NO health insurance or health insurance less than that provided to the aged under Medicare?

    A. 19%   B. 36%   C. 55%   D. 65%

14. According to the above passage, the one of the following types of health insurance which covered the SMALLEST number of Americans under age 65 was

    A. hospital insurance
    B. surgical insurance
    C. insurance for prescription drugs
    D. insurance for physician office or home visits

Questions 15-17.

DIRECTIONS: Questions 15 through 17 are to be answered SOLELY on the basis of the information contained in the following passage.

Statistical studies have demonstrated that disease and mortality rates are higher among the poor than among the more affluent members of our society. Periodic surveys conducted by the United States Public Health Service continue to document a higher prevalence of infectious and chronic diseases within low income families. While the basic life style and living conditions of the poor are to a considerable extent responsible for this less favorable health status, there are indications that the kind of health care received by the poor also plays a significant role. The poor are less likely to be aware of the concepts and practices of scientific medicine and less likely to seek health care when they need it. Moreover, they are discouraged from seeking adequate health care by the depersonalization, disorganization, and inadequate emphasis on preventive care which characterize the health care most often provided for them.

To achieve the objective of better health care for the poor, the following approaches have been suggested: encouraging the poor to seek preventive care as well as care for acute illness and to establish a lasting one-to-one relationship with a single physician who can treat the poor patient as a whole individual; sufficient financial subsidy to put the poor on an equal footing with *paying patients,* thereby giving them the opportunity to choose from among available health services providers; inducements to health services providers to establish public clinics in poverty areas; and legislation to provide for health education, earlier detection of disease, and coordinated health care.

15. According to the above passage, the one of the following which is a function of the United States Public Health Service is

    A. gathering data on the incidence of infectious diseases
    B. operating public health clinics in poverty areas lacking private physicians
    C. recommending legislation for the improvement of health care in the United States
    D. encouraging the poor to participate in programs aimed at the prevention of illness

16. According to the above passage, the one of the following which is MOST characteristic of the health care currently provided for the poor is that it

    A. aims at establishing clinics in poverty areas
    B. enables the poor to select the health care they want through the use of financial subsidies
    C. places insufficient stress on preventive health care
    D. over-emphasizes the establishment of a one-to-one relationship between physician and patient

16._____

17. The above passage IMPLIES that the poor lack the financial resources to

    A. obtain adequate health insurance coverage
    B. select from among existing health services
    C. participate in health education programs
    D. lobby for legislation aimed at improving their health care

17._____

Questions 18-20.

DIRECTIONS: Questions 18 through 20 are to be answered SOLELY on the basis of the information contained in the following passage.

The concept of *affiliation,* developed more than ten years ago, grew out of a series of studies which found evidence of faulty care, surgery of *questionable* value and other undesirable conditions in the city's municipal hospitals. The affiliation agreements signed shortly thereafter were designed to correct these deficiencies by assuring high quality medical care. In general, the agreements provided the staff and expertise of a voluntary hospital—sometimes connected with a medical school—to operate various services or, in some cases, all of the professional divisions of a specific municipal hospital. The municipal hospitals have paid for these services, which last year cost the city $200 million, the largest single expenditure of the Health and Hospitals Corporation. In addition, the municipal hospitals have provided to the voluntary hospitals such facilities as free space for laboratories and research. While some experts agree that affiliation has resulted in improvements in some hospital care, they contend that many conditions that affiliation was meant to correct still exist. In addition, accountability procedures between the Corporation and voluntary hospitals are said to be so inadequate that audits of affiliation contracts of the past five years revealed that there may be more than $200 million in charges for services by the voluntary hospitals which have not been fully substantiated. Consequently, the Corporation has proposed that future agreements provide accountability in terms of funds, services supplied, and use of facilities by the voluntary hospitals.

18. According to the above passage, *affiliation* may BEST be defined as an agreement whereby

    A. voluntary hospitals pay for the use of municipal hospital facilities
    B. voluntary and municipal hospitals work to eliminate duplication of services
    C. municipal hospitals pay voluntary hospitals for services performed
    D. voluntary and municipal hospitals transfer patients to take advantage of specialized services

18._____

19. According to the above passage, the MAIN purpose for setting up the *affiliation* agreement was to

    A. supplement the revenues of municipal hospitals
    B. improve the quality of medical care in municipal hospitals
    C. reduce operating costs in municipal hospitals
    D. increase the amount of space available to municipal hospitals

20. According to the above passage, inadequate accountability procedures have resulted in

    A. unsubstantiated charges for services by the voluntary hospitals
    B. emphasis on research rather than on patient care in municipal hospitals
    C. unsubstantiated charges for services by the municipal hospitals
    D. economic losses to voluntary hospitals

Questions 21-25.

DIRECTIONS: Questions 21 through 25 are to be answered SOLELY on the basis of the information contained in the following passage.

The payment for medical services covered under the Outpatient Medical Insurance Plan (OMI) may be made, by OMI, directly to a physician or to the OMI patient. If the physician and the patient agree that the physician is to receive payment directly from OMI, the payment will be officially assigned to the physician; this is the assignment method. If payment is not assigned, the patient receives payment directly from OMI based on an itemized bill he submits, regardless of whether or not he has already paid his physician.

When a physician accepts assignment of the payment for medical services, he agrees that total charges will not be more than the allowed charge determined by the OMI carrier administering the program. In such cases, the OMI patient pays any unmet part of the $85 annual deductible, plus 10 percent of the remaining charges to the physician. In unassigned claims, the patient is responsible for the total amount charged by the physician. The patient will then be reimbursed by the program 90 percent of the allowed charges in excess of the annual deductible.

The rates of acceptance of assignments provide a measure of how many OMI patients are spared *administrative participation* in the program. Because physicians are free to accept or reject assignments, the rate in which assignments are made provide a general indication of the medical community's satisfaction with the OMI program, especially with the level of amounts paid by the program for specific services and the promptness of payment.

21. According to the above passage, in order for a physician to receive payment directly from OMI for medical services to an OMI patient, the physician would have to accept the assignment of payment, to have the consent of the patient, AND to

    A. submit to OMI a paid itemized bill
    B. collect from the patient 90% of the total bill
    C. collect from the patient the total amount of the charges for his services, a portion of which he will later reimburse the patient
    D. agree that his charges for services to the patient will not exceed the amount allowed by the program

22. According to the above passage, if a physician accepts assignment of payment, the patient pays

    A. the total amount charged by the physician and is reimbursed by the program for 90 percent of the allowed charges in excess of the applicable deductible
    B. any unmet part of the $85 annual deductible, plus 90 percent of the remaining charges
    C. the total amount charged by the physician and is reimbursed by the program for 10 percent of the allowed charges in excess of the $85 annual deductible
    D. any unmet part of the $85 annual deductible, plus 10 percent of the remaining charges

23. A physician has accepted the assignment of payment for charges to an OMI patient. The physician's charges, all of which are allowed under OMI, amount to $115. This is the first time the patient has been eligible for OMI benefits and the first time the patient has received services from this physician.
    According to the above passage, the patient must pay the physician

    A. $27   B. $76.50   C. $88   D. $103.50

24. In an unassigned claim, a physician's charges, all of which are allowed under OMI, amount to $165. The patient paid the physician the full amount of the bill.
    If this is the FIRST time the patient has been eligible for OMI benefits, he will receive from OMI a reimbursement of

    A. $72   B. $80   C. $85   D. $93

25. According to the above passage, if the rate of acceptance of assignments by physicians is high, it is LEAST appropriate to conclude that the medical community is generally satisfied with the

    A. supplementary medical insurance program
    B. levels of amounts paid to physicians by the program
    C. number of OMI patients being spared administrative participation in the program
    D. promptness of the program in making payment for services

KEY (CORRECT ANSWERS)

1. B	11. C	21. D
2. A	12. A	22. D
3. C	13. C	23. C
4. D	14. D	24. A
5. A	15. A	25. C
6. D	16. C	
7. B	17. B	
8. C	18. C	
9. B	19. B	
10. D	20. A	

ABILITY TO APPLY STATED LAWS, RULES AND REGULATIONS

EXAMINATION SECTION

TEST 1

DIRECTIONS: Each question or incomplete statement is followed by several suggested answers or completions. Select the one that BEST answers the question or completes the statement. *PRINT THE LETTER OF THE CORRECT ANSWER IN THE SPACE AT THE RIGHT.*

Questions 1-2.

DIRECTIONS: Questions 1 and 2 are to be answered on the basis of the following passage.

Effective January 1, 2022, employees who are entitled to be paid at an overtime minimum wage rate according to the terms of a state minimum wage order must be paid for overtime at a rate at least time and one-half of the appropriate regular minimum wage rate for non-overtime work. For the purpose of this policy statement, the term *appropriate regular minimum* wage rate means $10.05 per hour or a lower minimum wage rate established in accordance with the provisions of a state minimum wage order. OVERTIME MINIMUM WAGES MAY NOT BE OFFSET BY PAYMENTS IN EXCESS OF THE REGULAR MINIMUM RATE OR NON-OVERTIME WORK.

1. A worker who ordinarily works forty hours a week at an agreed wage of $12.00 an hour is required to work ten hours in excess of forty during a payroll week and is paid for the extra ten hours at his $12.00 per hour rate.
 Using the information contained in the above passage, it is BEST to conclude
 A. this was a correct application of the regulation
 B. this was an incorrect application of the regulation
 C. the employee was not underpaid because he or she agreed upon the wage rate
 D. the employee did not perform his job well

1._____

2. According to the information in the above passage, the employee in Question 1 was MOST likely underpaid at least
 A. $180.00 B. $30.75
 C. $60.00   D. not underpaid at all

2._____

Question 3.

DIRECTIONS: Question 3 is to be answered on the basis of the following passage.

The following guidelines establish a range of monetary assessments for various types of child labor violations. They are general in nature and may not cover every specific situation. In determining the appropriate monetary amount within the range shown, consideration will be given to the criteria enumerated in the statute, namely *the size of the employer's business, the good faith of the employer, the gravity of the violation, the history of previous violations, and the failure to comply with record keeping or other requirements.* For example, the penalty for a larger firm (25 or more employees) would tend to be in the higher range since such firms should have knowledge of the laws. The gravity of the violation would depend on such factors as the age of the minor, whether required to be in school, and the degree of exposure to the hazards of prohibited occupations. Failure to keep records of the hours of work of the minors would also have a bearing on the size of the penalty.

1. a. No employment certificate—child of employer (Sec. 131 or 132)
   b. No posted hours of work (Sect. 178)

   1st Violation - $0-$100
   2nd Violation - $100-$250
   3rd Violation - $250-$500

2. a. Invalid employment certificate, e.g., student non-factory rather than general for a 16 year old in non-factory work (Sec. 132)
   b. Maximum or prohibited hours—less than one half hour beyond limit on any day, occasional, no pattern. (Sec. 130. 2e, 131.3f, 170.1, 171.1, 170l2, 172.1, 173.1; Ed. L. 3227, 3228)

   1st Violation - $0-$100
   2nd Violation - $150-$250
   3rd Violation - $250-$500

3. a. No employment certificate. (Sec. 130.2e, 131.3f, 131, 132, 138; Ed. L. 3227, 3228; ACAL 35.01, 35.05)
   b. Maximum of prohibited hours – (1) less than one half hour beyond limit on regular basis, (2) more than one half hour beyond limit either occasional or on a regular basis (Sec. 130.2e, 131.3f, 170.1, 170.2, 172.1, 173.1;Ed. L. 3227, 3228)

   1st Violation - $100-$250
   2nd Violation - $250-$500
   3rd Violation - $400-$500

4. Prohibited Occupations—Hazardous Employment (Sec. 130.1, 131.3f, 131.2, 133)

   1st Violation - $300-$500
   2nd Violation - $400-$500
   3rd Violation - $400-$500

<u>COMPLIANCE CONFERENCE PRIOR TO ASSESSMENT OF PENALTY</u>
After a child labor violation is reported, a compliance conference will be scheduled affording the employer the opportunity to be heard on the reported violation. A determination regarding the assessment of a civil penalty will be made following the conference.

<u>RIGHT TO APPEAL</u>
If the employer is aggrieved by the determination following such conference, the employer has the right to appeal such determination within 60 days of the date of issuance to the Industrial Board of Appeals, 194 Washington Avenue, Albany, New York 12210 as prescribed by its Rules of Procedure.

3. According to the above passage, a firm with its third violation of child labor laws regarding no posted hours of work (Sec. 178) and prohibited occupations-hazardous employment would be fined
   A. $600$1,000
   B. $650
   C. $1,000
   D. cannot be determined from the information given

Question 4.

DIRECTIONS: Question 4 is to be answered on the basis of the following passage.

Section 198c.   <u>Benefits or Wage Supplements</u>

1. In addition to any other penalty or punishment otherwise prescribed by law, any employer who is party to an agreement to pay or provide benefits or wage supplements to employees or to a third party or fund for the benefit of employees and who fails, neglects, or refuses to pay the amount or amounts necessary to provide such benefits or furnish such supplements within thirty days after such payments are required to be made, shall be guilty of a misdemeanor, and upon conviction shall be punished as provided in Section One Hundred Ninety-Eight-a of this article. Where such employer is a corporation, the president, secretary treasurer, or officers exercising corresponding functions shall each be guilty of a misdemeanor.

2. As used in this section, the term *benefits* or *wage supplements* includes, but is not limited to, reimbursement for expenses; health, welfare, and retirement benefits; and vacation, separation or holiday pay.

4. According to the above passage, an employer who had agreed to furnish an employee with a car and then failed to provide a car is
   A. not guilty of a misdemeanor
   B. most likely guilty of a misdemeanor
   C. not affected by the above regulation
   D. guilty of a felony

Question 5.

DIRECTIONS: Question 5 is to be answered on the basis of the following passage.

Manual workers must be paid weekly and not later than seven calendar days after the end of the week in which the wages are earned. However, a manual worker employed by a non-profitmaking organization must be paid in accordance with the agreed terms of employment, but not less frequently than semi-monthly. A manual worker means a mechanic, workingman, or laborer. Railroad workers, other than executives, must be paid on or before Thursday of each week the wages earned during the seven day period ending on Tuesday of the preceding week. Commission sales personnel must be paid in accordance with the agreed terms of employment but not less frequently than once in each month and not later than the last day of the month following the month in which the money is earned. If the monthly payment of wages, salary, drawing account or commissions is substantial, then additional compensation such as incentive earnings may be paid less frequently than once in each month, but in no event later than the time provided in the employment agreement.

5. A non-executive railroad worker has not been paid for the previous week's work. It is Wednesday.
   According to the above passage, which of the following is TRUE?
   The above regulation
   A. was not violated since the ending period is the following Tuesday
   B. was violated
   C. was not violated since the employee could be paid on Thursday
   D. does not apply in this case

5._____

Questions 6.

DIRECTIONS: Question 6 is to be answered on the basis of the following passage.

No deductions may be made from wages except deductions authorized by law, or which are authorized in writing by the employee and are for the employee's benefit. Authorized deductions include payments for insurance premiums, pensions, U.S. bonds, and union dues, as well as similar payments for the benefit of the employee. An employer may not make any payment by separate transaction unless such charge or payment is permitted as a deduction from wages. Examples of illegal deductions or charges include payments by the employee for spoilage, breakage, cash shortages or losses, and cost and maintenance of required uniforms.

6. An employee working on a cash register is short $40 at the end of his shift. The $40 is deducted from his wages.
   According to the above passage, the deduction is
   A. legal because it is legal to deduct cash losses
   B. legal because the employee is at fault
   C. illegal because the employee was not told of the deduction in advance
   D. illegal

6._____

Questions 7-8.

DIRECTIONS: Questions 7 and 8 are to be answered on the basis of the following passage.

No employee shall be paid a wage at a rate less than the rate at which an employee of the opposite sex in the same establishment is paid for equal work on a job, the performance of which requires equal skill, effort, and responsibility, and which is performed under similar working conditions, except where payment is made pursuant to a differential based on:
   a. A system which measures earnings by quantity or quality of production
   b. A merit system
   c. A seniority system; or
   d. Any other factor other than sex.

Any violation of the above is illegal.

7. A woman working in a factory on a piece-rate system as a sewing machine operator received less pay than a male sewing machine operator who finished more items.
   According to the above regulation, this is
   A. legal
   B. illegal
   C. legal, but not ethical
   D. no conclusion can be made from the information given

   7.____

8. A male worker is in the same job title as a female worker. The male worker has been employed by the firm for three years, the female for two.
   Using the regulation stated above, if the male worker is paid more than the female worker, the action is
   A. legal
   B. illegal
   C. legal, but not ethical
   D. no conclusion can be made from the information given

   8.____

Question 9.

DIRECTIONS: Question 9 is to be answered on the basis of the following passage.

Section 162. <u>Time Allowed for Meals</u>

1. Every person employed in or in connection with a factory shall be allowed at least sixty minutes for the noon day meal.

2. Every person employed in or in connection with a mercantile or other establishment or occupation coming under the provisions of this chapter shall be allowed at least forty-five minutes for the noon day meal, except as in this chapter otherwise provided.

3. Every person employed for a period or shift starting before noon and continuing later than seven o'clock in the evening shall be allowed an additional meal period of at least twenty minutes between five and seven o'clock in the evening.

4. Every person employed for a period or shift of more than six hours starting between the hours of one o'clock in the afternoon and six o'clock in the morning, shall be allowed at least sixty minutes for a meal period when employed in or in connection with a factory, and forty-five minutes for a meal period when employed in or in connection with a mercantile or other establishment or occupation coming under the provision of this chapter, at a time midway between the beginning and end of such employment.

5. The commissioner may permit a shorter time to be fixed for meal periods than hereinbefore provided. The permit therefore shall be in writing and shall be kept conspicuously posted in the main entrance of the establishment. Such permit may be revoked at any time.

In administering this statute, the Department applies the following interpretations and guidelines:

Employee Coverage: Section 162 applies to every person in any establishment or occupation covered by the Labor Law. Accordingly, all categories of workers are covered, including white collar management staff.

Shorter Meal Periods: The Department will permit a shorter meal period of not less than 30 minutes as a matter of course, without application by the employer, so long as there is no indication of hardship to employees. A meal period of not less than 20 minutes will be permitted only in special or unusual cases after investigation and issuance of a special permit.

9. An employee is given twenty minutes for lunch
According to the information given in the above passage, the employer
   A. is in violation
   B. is not in violation
   C. should be fined $250
   D. no conclusion can be made from the information given

Question 10.

DIRECTIONS: Question 10 is to be answered on the basis of the following passage.

An employee shall not be obliged to incur expenses in the arrangement whereby the employee's wages or salary are directly deposited in a bank or financial institution or in the withdrawal of such wages or salary from the bank or financial institution. Some examples of expenses are as follows:

1. A service charge, per check charge, or administrative or processing charge.
2. Carfare in order to get to the bank or financial institution to withdraw wages.

An employee shall not be obliged to lose a substantial amount of uncompensated time in order to withdraw wages from a bank or financial institution. Although the employer is not required to provide employees with paid time in which to withdraw such monies, the Department has held that the employer should provide for the loss of time when the employee requires more than 15 minutes to withdraw wages. Such time includes travel time to and from, as well as actual time spent at the bank or financial institution in withdrawing such monies. The loss of such time without compensation constitutes a difficulty.

The withdrawal of wages may not interfere with an employee's meal period to the extent that it decreases the meal period to less than 30 minutes. Thus, although the time required for withdrawal of wages may be 15 minutes or less, the loss of even 8 or 9 minutes from a thirty minute meal period creates a difficulty.

10. An employee is unable to withdraw wages at any time other than her lunch break. She needs twenty minutes to withdraw wages and has a forty-five minute lunch break.
    According to the information contained in the above passage, the employer
    A. is in violation
    B. is not in violation
    C. should be fined $250
    D. no conclusion can be made from the information given

10.____

KEY (CORRECT ANSWERS)

1. B   6. D
2. B   7. A
3. D   8. A
4. B   9. D
5. C   10. A

SOLUTIONS

1. The answer is choice B. According to the passage, the employee should have been paid "at a rate at least time and one half of the appropriate regular <u>minimum wage rate</u> for non-overtime work." Remember, it's important to consider only what has been given in the reading passage. Choice C is incorrect because it is illegal in this case to agree on something other than the law. Minimum standards are set by law so that employers cannot coerce, or otherwise persuade, employees to work at less than what is deemed fair. It could be argued that this is outside knowledge, but if you think about it, it's only common sense. Why bother having a minimum wage law, or minimum rates for overtime, or child labor laws if someone can just sign away his or her rights when an employer asks him or her to? If you didn't know this, you could still have eliminated this choice because the passage says, "ordinarily works 40 hours at an agreed wage of $12.00 per hour." The wording implies that this was agreed on for the <u>normal</u> work week.

2. The answer is choice B. The employee needs to be paid at a rate of time and a half. The employee has worked an extra ten hours at the hourly rate of $12.00 an hour. The passage states that the employee must be paid "at least time and one half of the appropriate regular minimum wage rate for non-overtime work." Minimum wage is given as $10.05 per hour. Time and a half of that would be $10.05 times 1.5, or $15.075 per hour. This employee is paid only $12.00 per hour for each hour of overtime. That's $3.075 less for each of the ten hours over forty hours, or a total of $30.75 less than he should have been paid. (10 × $3.075 = $30.75) You may have read the passage incorrectly, and thought the employee should have been paid time and a half on the $12.00 wage, but the passage does not state this. It states that the minimum payment is time and a half on <u>minimum hourly wage</u>, not on the employee's current wage rate. If you assumed the employee should have been paid $18.00 an hour, you probably would have picked choice C. Very tricky question. NOTE: The employee could have been paid less than half the minimum wage under special circumstances. Since there is nothing to indicate that the special circumstances apply, and since the question stem says "most likely," choice B is still considered the best choice.

3. The answer is choice D. This is another tricky question. The passage states, "The following guidelines establish a range of monetary assessments for various types of violations. They are general in nature and <u>may not cover every specific situation</u>. In determining the appropriate monetary amount within the range shown, considered will be given to the criteria enumerated in the statute...." The passage then goes on to list all of, the various possibilities. We don't know the circumstances, so choice D is the safest choice. If the question stem had been phrased "would most likely be fined," a case might possibly have been made for a different answer. The way it stands, choice D is the best choice because we can't say what, the fine <u>definitely</u> <u>would be</u>.

4. The answer is choice B. The last sentence states that "the term benefits or wage supplements includes <u>but is not limited to</u>...." This, coupled with the wording of the first paragraph, would mean that there is a good possibility the broken agreement would be judged a misdemeanor.

5. The answer is choice C. This is directly supported by the fourth sentence.

6. The answer is choice D. The last sentence states that "examples of <u>illegal deductions</u> or charges include payments by the employee for spoilage, breakage, <u>cash shortages</u> or losses...."

7. The answer is choice A. The key here is the phrase <u>piece-rate system</u>. The passage states that one of the exceptions is "a system which measures earnings by quantity or quality of production." That's piecework where extra pay may be given for extra production or effort. It's logical—and not too much—to assume that the man was paid more because he finished more items.

8. The answer is choice A. The passage states that one of the exceptions is a seniority system. The question stem says that the man had worked there for three years while the woman had only worked there for two years.

9. The answer is choice D. The last sentence of the passage states that "a meal period of not less than twenty minutes will be permitted only in special or unusual cases after investigation and issuance of the special permit." Since we don't know the circumstances, we can't <u>definitely</u> say the employer is or is not in violation.

10. The answer is choice A. The next to last sentence of the passage states that "the withdrawal of wages may not interfere with an employee's meal period to the extent that it decreases the meal period to less than twenty minutes." The employee can only withdraw wages during her meal period. If the employee has a forty-five minute lunch break, and needs twenty minutes to withdraw funds, then she only has twenty-five minutes for lunch, which the passage states is not sufficient.

REPORT WRITING

EXAMINATION SECTION

TEST 1

DIRECTIONS: Each question or incomplete statement is followed by several suggested answers or completions. Select the one that BEST answers the question or completes the statement. *PRINT THE LETTER OF THE CORRECT ANSWER IN THE SPACE AT THE RIGHT.*

1. Following are six steps that should be taken in the course of report preparation:
   I. Outlining the material for presentation in the report
   II. Analyzing and interpreting the facts
   III. Analyzing the problem
   IV. Reaching conclusions
   V. Writing, revising, and rewriting the final copy
   VI. Collecting data

   According to the principles of good report writing, the CORRECT order in which these steps should be taken is:
   A. VI, III, II, I, IV, V
   B. III, VI, II, IV, I, V
   C. III, VI, II, I, IV, V
   D. VI, II, III, IV, I, V

   1.____

2. Following are three statements concerning written reports:
   I. Clarity is generally more essential in oral reports than in written reports.
   II. Short sentences composed of simple words are generally preferred to complex sentences and difficult words.
   III. Abbreviations may be used whenever they are customary and will not distract the attention of the reader.

   Which of the following choices correctly classifies the above statements in to those which are valid and those which are not valid?
   A. I and II are valid, but III is not valid
   B. I is valid, but II and III are not valid.
   C. II and III are valid, but I is not valid.
   D. III is valid, but I and II are not valid.

   2.____

3. In order to produce a report written in a style that is both understandable and effective, an investigator should apply the principles of unit, coherence, and emphasis.
   The one of the following which is the BEST example of the principle of coherence is
   A. interlinking sentences so that thoughts flow smoothly
   B. having each sentence express a single idea to facilitate comprehension
   C. arranging important points in prominent positions so they are not overlooked
   D. developing the main idea fully to insure complete consideration

   3.____

103

4. Assume that a supervisor is preparing a report recommending that a standard work procedure be changed.
   Of the following, the MOST important information that he should include in this report is
   A. a complete description of the present procedure
   B. the details and advantages of the recommended procedure
   C. the type and amount of retraining needed
   D. the percentage of men who favor the change

5. When you include in your report on an inspection some information which you have obtained from other individuals, it is MOST important that
   A. this information have no bearing on the work these other people are performing
   B. you do not report as fact the opinions of other individuals
   C. you keep the source of the information confidential
   D. you do not tell the other individuals that their statements will be included in your report

6. Before turning in a report of an investigator of an accident, you discover some additional information you did not know about when you wrote the report.
   Whether or not you re-write your report to include this additional information should depend MAINLY on the
   A. source of this additional information
   B. established policy covering the subject matter of the report
   C. length of the report and the time it would take you to re-write it
   D. bearing this additional information will have on the conclusions in the report

7. The MOST desirable *first* step in the planning of a written report is to
   A. ascertain what necessary information is readily available in the files
   B. outline the methods you will employ to get the necessary information
   C. determine the objectives and uses of the report
   D. estimate the time and cost required to complete the report

8. In writing a report, the practice of taking up the least important points and the most important points last is a
   A. *good* technique since the final points made in a report will make the greatest impression on the reader
   B. *good* technique since the material is presented in a more logical manner and will lead directly to the conclusions
   C. *poor* technique since the reader's time is wasted by having to review irrelevant information before finishing the report
   D. *poor* technique since it may cause the reader to lose interest in the report and arrive at incorrect conclusions about the report

3 (#1)

9. Which one of the following serves as the BEST guideline for you to follow for effective written reports?
Keep sentences
   A. short and limit sentences to one thought
   B. short and use as many thoughts as possible
   C. long and limit sentences to one thought
   D. long and use as many thoughts as possible

9._____

10. One method by which a supervisor might prepare written reports to management is to begin with the conclusions, results, or summary, and to follow this with the supporting data.
The BEST reason why management may *prefer* this form of report is that
   A. management lacks the specific training to understand the data
   B. the data completely supports the conclusions
   C. time is saved by getting to the conclusions of the report first
   D. the data contains all the information that is required for making the conclusions

10._____

11. When making written reports, it is MOST important that they be
   A. well-worded   B. accurate as to the facts
   C. brief   D. submitted immediately

11._____

12. Of the following, the MOST important reason for a supervisor to prepare good written reports is that
   A. a supervisor is rated on the quality of his reports
   B. decisions are often made on the basis of the reports
   C. such reports take less time for superiors to review
   D. such reports demonstrate efficiency of department operations

12._____

13. Of the following, the BEST test of a good report is whether it
   A. provides the information needed
   B. shows the good sense of the writer
   C. is prepared according to a proper format
   D. is grammatical and neat

13._____

14. When a supervisor writes a report, he can BEST show that he has a understanding of the subject of the report by
   A. including necessary facts and omitting nonessential details
   B. using statistical data
   C. giving his conclusions but not the data on which they are based
   D. using a technical vocabulary

14._____

15. Suppose you and another supervisor on the same level are assigned to work together on a report. You disagree strongly with one of the recommendations the other supervisor wants to include in the report but you cannot change his views.

15._____

Of the following, it would be BEST that
- A. you refuse to accept responsibility for the report
- B. you ask that someone else be assigned to this project to replace you
- C. each of you state his own ideas about this recommendation in the report
- D. you give in to the other supervisor's opinion for the sake of harmony

16. Standardized forms are often provided for submitting reports. 16._____
Of the following, the MOST important advantage of using standardized forms for reports is that
- A. they take less time to prepare than individually written reports
- B. the person making the report can omit information he considers unimportant
- C. the responsibility for preparing these reports can be turned over to subordinates
- D. necessary information is less likely to be omitted

17. A report which may BEST be classed as a *periodic* report is one which 17._____
- A. requires the same type of information at regular intervals
- B. contains detailed information which is to be retained in permanent records
- C. is prepared whenever a special situation occurs
- D. lists information in graphic form

18. In the writing of reports or letters, the ideas presented in a paragraph are usually of unequal importance and require varying degrees of emphasis. 18._____
All of the following are methods of placing extra stress on an idea EXCEPT
- A. repeating it in a number of forms
- B. placing it in the middle of the paragraph
- C. placing it either at the beginning or at the end of a paragraph
- D. underlining it

Questions 19-25.

DIRECTIONS: Questions 19 through 25 concern the subject of report writing and are based on the information and incidents described in the following paragraph. (In answering these questions, assume that the facts and incidents in the paragraph are true.)

On December 15, at 8 A.M., seven Laborers reported to Foreman Joseph Meehan in the Greenbranch Yard in Queens. Meehan instructed the men to load some 50-pound boxes of books on a truck for delivery to an agency building in Brooklyn. Meehan told the men that, because the boxes were rather heavy, two men should work together, helping each other lift and load each box. Since Michael Harper, one of the Laborers, was without a partner, Meehan helped him with the boxes for a while. When Meehan was called to the telephone in a nearby building, however, Harper decided to lift a box himself. He appeared able to lift the box, but, as he got the box halfway up, he cried out that he had a sharp pain in his back. Another Laborer, Jorge Ortiz, who was passing by, ran over to help Harper put the box down. Harper suddenly dropped the box, which fell on Ortiz' right foot. By this time, Meehan had come out of the building. He immediately helped get the box off Ortiz' foot and had both men lie down. Meehan covered the men with blankets and called an ambulance, which arrived a half hour later. At the hospital, the doctor said that the X-ray results showed that Ortiz' right foot was broken in three places.

19. What would be the BEST term to use in a report describing the injury of Jorge Ortiz?
    A. Strain B. Fracture C. Hernia D. Hemorrhage

    19._____

20. Which of the following would be the MOST accurate summary for the Foreman to put in his report of the incident?
    A. Ortiz attempted to help Harper carry a box which was too heavy for one person, but Harper dropped it before Ortiz got there.
    B. Ortiz tried to help Harper carry a box but Harper got a pain in his back and accidentally dropped the box on Ortiz' foot.
    C. Harper refused to follow Meehan's orders and lifted a box too heavy for him; he deliberately dropped it when Ortiz tried to help him carry it.
    D. Harper lifted a box and felt a pain in his back; Ortiz tried to help Harper put the box down but Harper accidentally dropped it on Ortiz' foot.

    20._____

21. One of the Laborers at the scene of the accident was asked his version of the incident.
    Which information obtained from this witness would be LEAST important for including in the accident report?
    A. His opinion as to the cause of the accident
    B. How much of the accident he saw
    C. His personal opinion of the victims
    D. His name and address

    21._____

22. What should be the MAIN objective of writing a report about the incident described in the above paragraph? To
    A. describe the important elements in the accident situation
    B. recommend that such Laborers as Ortiz be advised not to interfere in another's work unless given specific instructions
    C. analyze the problems occurring when there are not enough workers to perform a certain task
    D. illustrate the hazards involved in performing routine everyday tasks

    22._____

23. Which of the following is information *missing* from the above passage but which *should* be included in a report of the incident? The
    A. name of the Laborer's immediate supervisor
    B. contents of the boxes
    C. time at which the accident occurred
    D. object or action that caused the injury to Ortiz' foot

    23._____

24. According to the description of the incident, the accident occurred because
    A. Ortiz attempted to help Harper who resisted his help
    B. Harper failed to follow instructions given him by Meehan
    C. Meehan was not supervising his men as closely as he should have
    D. Harper was not strong enough to carry the box once he lifted it

    24._____

25. Which of the following is MOST important for a foreman to avoid when writing up an official accident report? 25.____
    A. Using technical language to describe equipment involved in the accident
    B. Putting in details which might later be judged unnecessary
    C. Giving an opinion as to conditions that contributed to the accident
    D. Recommending discipline for employees who, in his opinion, caused the accident

---

KEY (CORRECT ANSWERS)

1. B	11. B
2. C	12. B
3. A	13. A
4. B	14. A
5. B	15. C
6. D	16. D
7. C	17. A
8. D	18. B
9. A	19. B
10. C	20. D

21. C
22. A
23. C
24. B
25. D

TEST 2

DIRECTIONS: Each question or incomplete statement is followed by several suggested answers or completions. Select the one that BEST answers the question or completes the statement. *PRINT THE LETTER OF THE CORRECT ANSWER IN THE SPACE AT THE RIGHT.*

1. Lieutenant X is preparing a report to submit to his commanding officer in order to get approval of a plan of operation he has developed.
   The report starts off with the statement of the problem and continues with the details of the problem. It contains factual information gathered with the help of field and operational personnel. It contains a final conclusion and recommendation for action. The recommendation is supplemented by comments from other precinct staff members on how the recommendations will affect their areas of responsibility. The report also includes directives and general orders ready for the commanding officer's signature. In addition, it has two statements of objections presented by two precinct staff members.
   Which one of the following, if any, is either an item that Lieutenant X should have included in his report and which is not mentioned above, or is an item which Lieutenant X improperly did include in his report?
   A. Considerations of alternative courses of action and their consequences should have been covered in the report.
   B. The additions containing undocumented objections to the recommended course of action should not have been included as part of the report.
   C. A statement on the qualifications of Lieutenant X, which would support his expertness in the field under consideration, should have been included in the report.
   D. The directives and general orders should not have been prepared and included in the report until the commanding officer had approved the recommendations.
   E. None of the above, since Lieutenant X's report was both proper and complete.

1.____

2. During a visit to a section, the district supervisor criticizes the method being used by the assistant foreman to prepare a certain report and orders him to modify the method. This change ordered by the district supervisor is in direct conflict with the specific orders of the foreman.
   In this situation, it would be BEST for the assistant foreman to
   A. change the method and tell the foreman about the change at the first opportunity
   B. change the method and rely on the district supervisor to notify the foreman
   C. report the matter to the foreman and delay the preparation of the report
   D. ask the district supervisor to discuss the matter with the foreman but use the old method for the time being

2.____

3. A department officer should realize that the MOST usual reason for writing a report is to
    A. give orders and follow up their execution
    B. establish a permanent record
    C. raise questions
    D. supply information

4. A very important report which is being prepared by a department officer will soon be due on the desk of the district supervisor. No typing help is available at this time for the officer.
   For the officer to write out this report in longhand in such a situation would be
    A. *bad*; such a report would not make the impression a typed report would
    B. *good*; it is important to get the report in on time
    C. *bad*; the district supervisor should not be required to read longhand reports
    D. *good*; it would call attention to the difficult conditions under which this section must work

5. In a well-written report, the length of each paragraph in the report should be
    A. varied according to the content
    B. not over 300 words
    C. pretty nearly the same
    D. gradually longer as the report is developed and written

6. A clerk in the headquarters office complains to you about the way in which you are filing out a certain report.
   It would be BEST for you to
    A. tell the clerk that you are following official procedures in filling out the report
    B. ask to be referred to the clerk's superior
    C. ask the clerk exactly what is wrong with the way in which you are filling out the report
    D. tell the clerk that you are following the directions of the district supervisor

7. The use of an outline to help in writing a report is
    A. *desirable*, in order to insure good organization and coverage
    B. *necessary*, so it can be used as an introduction to the report itself
    C. *undesirable*, since it acts as a straightjacket and may result in an unbalanced report
    D. *desirable*, if you know your immediate supervisor reads reports with extreme care and attention

8. It is advisable that a department officer do his paper work and report writing as soon as he has completed an inspection MAINLY because
    A. there are usually deadlines to be met
    B. it insures a steady work-flow
    C. he may not have time for this later
    D. the facts are then freshest in his mind

9. Before you turn in a report you have written of an investigation that you have made, you discover some additional information you didn't know about before. Whether or not you re-write the report to include this additional information should depend MAINLY on the
    A. amount of time remaining before the report is due
    B. established policy of the department covering the subject matter of the report
    C. bearing this information will have on the conclusions of the report
    D. number of people who will eventually review the report

10. When a supervisory officer submits a periodic report to the district supervisor, he should realize that the CHIEF importance of such a report is that it
    A. is the principal method of checking on the efficiency of the supervisor and his subordinates
    B. is something to which frequent reference will be made
    C. eliminates the need for any personal follow-up or inspection by higher echelons
    D. permits the district supervisor to exercise his functions of direction, supervision, and control better

11. Conclusions and recommendations are usually placed at the end rather than at the beginning of a report because
    A. the person preparing the report may decide to change some of the conclusions and recommendations before he reaches the end of the report
    B. they are the most important part of the report
    C. they can be judged better by the person to whom the report is sent after he reads the facts and investigators which come earlier in the report
    D. they can be referred to quickly when needed without reading the rest of the report

12. The use of the same method of record-keeping and reporting by all agency sections is
    A. *desirable*, MAINLY because it saves time in section operations
    B. *undesirable*, MAINLY because it kills the initiative of the individual section foreman
    C. *desirable*, MAINLY because it will be easier for the administrator to evaluate and compare section operations
    D. *undesirable*, MAINLY because operations vary from section to section and uniform record-keeping and reporting is not appropriate

13. The GREATEST benefit the section officer will have from keeping complete and accurate records and reports of section operations is that
    A. he will find it easier to run his section efficiently
    B. he will need less equipment
    C. he will need less manpower
    D. the section will run smoothly when he is out

14. You have prepared a report to your superior and are ready to send it forward. 14.____
But on re-reading it, you think some parts are not clearly expressed and your
superior ay have difficulty getting your point.
Of the following, it would be BEST for you to
    A. give the report to one of your men to read, and if he has no trouble
       understanding it send it through
    B. forward the report and call your superior the next day to ask whether it
       was all right
    C. forward the report as is; higher echelons should be able to understand
       any report prepared by a section officer
    D. do the report over, re-writing the sections you are in doubt about

15. The BEST of the following statements concerning reports is that 15.____
    A. a carelessly written report may give the reader an impression of
       inaccuracy
    B. correct grammar and English are unimportant if the main facts are given
    C. every man should be required to submit a daily work report
    D. the longer and more wordy a report is, the better it will read

16. In writing a report, the question of whether or not to include certain material 16.____
could be determined BEST by considering the
    A. amount of space the material will occupy in the report
    B. amount of time to be spent in gathering the material
    C. date of the material
    D. value of the material to the superior who will read the report

17. Suppose you are submitting a fairly long report to your superior. 17.____
The one of the following sections that should come FIRST in this report is a
    A. description of how you gathered material
    B. discussion of possible objections to your recommendations
    C. plan of how your recommendations can be put into practice
    D. statement of the problem dealt with

Questions 18-20.

DIRECTIONS: A foreman is asked to write a report on the incident described in the following
passage. Answer Questions 18 through 20 based on the following information.

On March 10, Henry Moore, a laborer, was in the process of transferring some equipment
from the machine shop to the third floor. He was using a dolly to perform this task and, as he
was wheeling the material through the machine shop, laborer Bob Greene called to him. As
Henry turned to respond to Bob, he jammed the dolly into Larry Mantell's leg, knocking Larry
down in the process and causing the heavy drill that Larry was holding to fall on Larry's foot.
Larry started rubbing his foot and then, infuriated, jumped up and punched Henry in the jaw.
The force of the blow drove Henry's head back against the wall. Henry did not fight back; he
appeared to be dazed. An ambulance was called to take Henry to the hospital, and the
ambulance attendant told the foreman that it appeared likely that Henry had suffered a
concussion. Larry's injuries consisted of some bruises, but he refused medical attention.

18. An adequate report of the above incident should give as minimum information the names of the persons involved, the names of the witnesses, the date and the time that each event took place, and the
    A. names of the ambulance attendants
    B. names of all the employees working in the machine shop
    C. location where the accident occurred
    D. nature of the previous safety training each employee had been given

    18.____

19. The only one of the following which is NOT a fact is
    A. Bob called to Henry
    B. Larry suffered a concussion
    C. Larry rubbed his foot
    D. the incident took place in the machine shop

    19.____

20. Which of the following would be the MOST accurate summary of the incident for the foreman to put in his report of the accident?
    A. Larry Mantell punched Henry Moore because a drill fell on his foot and he was angry. Then Henry fell and suffered a concussion.
    B. Henry Moore accidentally jammed a dolly into Larry Mantell's foot, knocking Larry down. Larry punched Henry, pushing him into the wall and causing him to bang his head against the wall.
    C. Bob Greene called Henry Moore. A dolly than jammed into Larry Mantell and knocked him down. Larry punched Henry who tripped and suffered some bruises. An ambulance was called.
    D. A drill fell on Larry Mantell's foot. Larry jumped up suddenly and punched Henry Moore and pushed him into the wall. Henry may have suffered a concussion as a result of falling.

    20.____

Questions 21-25.

DIRECTIONS: Questions 21 through 25 are to be answered ONLY on the basis of the information provided in the following passage.

A written report is a communication of information from one person to another. It is an account of some matter especially investigated, however routine that matter may be. The ultimate basis of any good written report is facts, which become known through observation and verification. Good written reports may seem to be no more than general ideas and opinions. However, in such cases, the facts leading to these opinions were gathered, verified, and reported earlier, and the opinions are dependent upon these facts. Good style, proper form, and emphasis cannot make a good written report out of unreliable information and bad judgment; but, on the other hand, solid investigation and brilliant thinking are not likely to become very useful until they are effectively communicated to others. If a person's work calls for written reports, then his work is often no better than his written reports.

21. Based on the information in the above passage, it can be concluded that opinions expressed in a report should be
    A. based on facts which are gathered and reported
    B. emphasized repeatedly when they result from a special investigation
    C. kept to a minimum
    D. separated from the body of the report

    21._____

22. In the above passage, the one of the following which is mentioned as a way of establishing facts is
    A. authority
    B. communication
    C. reporting
    D. verification

    22._____

23. According to the above passage, the characteristic shared by ALL written reports is that they are
    A. accounts of routine matters
    B. transmissions of information
    C. reliable and logical
    D. written in proper form

    23._____

24. Which of the following conclusions can logically be drawn from the information given in the above passage?
    A. Brilliant thinking can make up for unreliable information in a report.
    B. One method of judging an individual's work is the quality of the written reports he is required to submit.
    C. Proper form and emphasis can make a good report out of unreliable information.
    D. Good written reports that seem to be no more than general ideas should be rewritten.

    24._____

25. Which of the following suggested titles would be MOST appropriate for this passage?
    A. Gathering and Organizing Facts
    B. Techniques of Observation
    C. Nature and Purpose of Reports
    D. Reports and Opinions: Differences and Similarities

    25._____

KEY (CORRECT ANSWERS)

1.	A	11.	C
2.	A	12.	C
3.	D	13.	A
4.	B	14.	D
5.	A	15.	A
6.	C	16.	D
7.	A	17.	D
8.	D	18.	C
9.	C	19.	B
10.	D	20.	B

21. A
22. D
23. B
24. B
25. C

TEST 3

DIRECTIONS: Each question or incomplete statement is followed by several suggested answers or completions. Select the one that BEST answers the question or completes the statement. *PRINT THE LETTER OF THE CORRECT ANSWER IN THE SPACE AT THE RIGHT.*

Questions 1-5.

DIRECTIONS: The following is an accident report similar to those used in departments for reporting accidents. Questions 1 through 5 are be answered using ONLY the information given in this report.

ACCIDENT REPORT

FROM: John Doe	DATE OF REPORT: June 23	
TITLE: Sanitation Worker		
DATE OF ACCIDENT: June 22 time 3 AM PM	CITY: Metropolitan	
PLACE: 1489 Third Avenue		
VEHICLE NO. 1	VEHICLE NO. 2	
OPERATOR: John Doe, Sanitation Worker Title	OPERATOR: Richard Roe	
VEHICLE CODE NO: 14-238	ADDRESS: 498 High Street	
LICENSE NO.: 0123456	OWNER: Henry Roe ADDRESS:786 E.83 St.	LIC. NO.: 5N1492
DESCRIPTION OF ACCIDENT: Light green Chevrolet sedan while trying to pass drove in to rear side of sanitation truck which had stopped to collect garbage. No one was injured but there was property damage.		
NATURE OF DAMAGE TO PRIVATE VEHICLE: Right front fender crushed, bumper bent		
DAMAGE TO CITY VEHICLE: Front of left rear fender pushed in. Paint scraped.		
NAME OF WITNESS: Frank Brown	ADDRESS: 48 Kingsway	
SIGNATURE OF PERSON MAKING THIS REPORT *John Doe*	BADGE NO.: 428	

1. Of the following, the one which has been omitted from this accident report is the
   A. location of the accident
   B. drivers of the vehicles involved
   C. traffic situation at the time of the accident
   D. owners of the vehicles involved

1.____

2. The address of the driver of Vehicle No. 1 is not required because he
   A. is employed by the department
   B. is not the owner of the vehicle
   C. reported the accident
   D. was injured in the accident

2.____

3. The report indicates that the driver of Vehicle No. 2 was PROBABLY
   A. passing on the wrong side of the truck
   B. not wearing his glasses
   C. not injured in the accident
   D driving while intoxicated

3.____

4. The number of people *specifically* referred to in this report is
   A. 3   B. 4   C. 5   D. 6

5. The license number of Vehicle No. 1 is
   A. 428   B. 5N1492   C. 14-238   D. 0123456

6. In a report of unlawful entry into department premises, it is LEAST important to include the
   A. estimated value of the property missing
   B. general description of the premises
   C. means used to get into the premises
   D. time and date of entry

7. In a report of an accident, it is LEAST important to include the
   A. name of the insurance company of the person injured in the accident
   B. probable cause of the accident
   C. time and place of the accident
   D. names and addresses of all witnesses of the accident

8. Of the following, the one which is NOT required in the preparation of a weekly functional expense report is the
   A. hourly distribution of the time by proper heading in accordance with the actual work performed
   B. signatures of officers not involved in the preparation of the report
   C. time records of the men who appear on the payroll of the respective locations
   D. time records of men working in other districts assigned to this location

KEY (CORRECT ANSWERS)

1.	C	5.	D
2.	A	6.	B
3.	C	7.	A
4.	B	8.	B

PREPARING WRITTEN MATERIAL

PARAGRAPH REARRANGEMENT
COMMENTARY

The sentences that follow are in scrambled order. You are to rearrange them in proper order and indicate the letter choice containing the correct answer at the space at the right.

Each group of sentences in this section is actually a paragraph presented in scrambled order. Each sentence in the group has a place in that paragraph; no sentence is to be left out. You are to read each group of sentences and decide upon the best order in which to put the sentences so as to form a well-organized paragraph.

The questions in this section measure the ability to solve a problem when all the facts relevant to its solution are not given.

More specifically, certain positions of responsibility and authority require the employee to discover connection between events sometimes, apparently, unrelated. In order to do this, the employee will find it necessary to correctly infer that unspecified events have probably occurred or are likely to occur. This ability becomes especially important when action must be taken on incomplete information.

Accordingly, these questions require competitors to choose among several suggested alternatives, each of which presents a different sequential arrangement of the events. Competitors must choose the MOST logical of the suggested sequences.

In order to do so, they may be required to draw on general knowledge to infer missing concepts or events that are essential to sequencing the given events. Competitors should be careful to infer only what is essential to the sequence. The plausibility of the wrong alternatives will always require the inclusion of unlikely events or of additional chains of events which are NOT essential to sequencing the given events.

It's very important to remember that you are looking for the best of the four possible choices, and that the best choice of all may not even be one of the answers you're given to choose from.

There is no one right way to solve these problems. Many people have found it helpful to first write out the order of the sentences, as they would have arranged them, on their scrap paper before looking at the possible answers. If their optimum answer is there, this can save them some time. If it isn't, this method can still give insight into solving the problem. Others find it most helpful to just go through each of the possible choices, contrasting each as they go along. You should use whatever method feels comfortable and works for you.

While most of these types of questions are not that difficult, we've added a higher percentage of the difficult type, just to give you more practice. Usually there are only one or two questions on this section that contain such subtle distinctions that you're unable to answer confidently. And you then may find yourself stuck deciding between two possible choices, neither of which you're sure about.

EXAMINATION SECTION
TEST 1

DIRECTIONS: The sentences listed below are part of a meaningful paragraph, but they are not given in their proper order. You are to decide what would be the BEST order to put sentences to form a well-organized paragraph. Each sentence has a place in the paragraph; there are no extra sentences. *PRINT THE LETTER OF THE CORRECT ANSWER IN THE SPACE AT THE RIGHT.*

1. I. He came on a winter's eve.
    II. Akira came directly, breaking all tradition.
    III. He pounded on the door while a cold rain beat on the shuttered veranda, so at first Chie thought him only the wind.
    IV. Was that it?
    V. Had he followed form—had he asked his mother to speak to his father to approach a go-between—would Chie have been more receptive?
    The CORRECT answer is:
    A. II, IV, V, I, III   B. I, III, II, IV, V   C. V, IV, II, III, I   D. III, V, I, II, IV

1.____

2. I. We have an understanding.
    II. Either method comes down to the same thing: a matter of parental approval.
    III. If you give your consent, I become Naomi's husband.
    IV. Please don't judge my candidacy by the unseemliness of this proposal.
    V. I ask directly because the use of a go-between takes much time.
    The CORRECT answer is:
    A. III, IV, II, V, I   B. I, V, II, III, IV   C. I, IV, V, II, III   D. V, III, I, IV, II

2.____

3. I. Many relish the opportunity to buy presents because gift-giving offers a powerful means to build stronger bonds with one's closest peers.
    II. Aside from purchasing holiday gifts, most people regularly buy presents for other occasions throughout the year, including weddings, birthdays, anniversaries, graduations, and baby showers.
    III. Last year, Americans spent over $30 billion at retail stores in the month of December alone.
    IV. This frequent experience of gift-giving can engender ambivalent feelings in gift-givers.
    V. Every day, millions of shoppers hit the stores in full force—both online and on foot—searching frantically for the perfect gift.
    The CORRECT answer is:
    A. II, III, V, I, IV   B. IV, V, I, III, II   C. III, II, V, I, IV   D. V, III, II, IV, I

3.____

4. I. Why do gift-givers assume that gift price is closely linked to gift-recipients' feelings of appreciation?
    II. Perhaps givers believe that bigger (i.e., more expensive) gifts convey stronger signals of thoughtfulness and consideration.
    III. In this sense, gift-givers may be motivated to spend more money on a gift in order to send a "stronger signal" to their intended recipient.
    IV. According to Camerer (1988) and others, gift-giving represents a symbolic ritual, whereby gift-givers attempt to signal their positive attitudes toward the intended recipient and their willingness to invest resources in a future relationship.
    V. As for gift-recipients, they may not construe smaller and larger gifts as representing smaller and larger signals of thoughtfulness and consideration.
    The CORRECT answer is:
    A. V, III, II, IV, I   B. I, II, IV, III, V   C. IV, I, III, V, II   D. II, V, I, IV, III

4.____

5. I. But when the spider is not hungry, the stimulation of its hairs merely causes it to shake the touched limb.
    II. Touching this body hair produces one of two distinct reactions.
    III. The entire body of a tarantula, especially its legs, is thickly clothed with hair.
    IV. Some of it is short and wooly, some long and stiff.
    V. When the spider is hungry, it responds with an immediate and swift attack.
    The CORRECT answer is:
    A. IV, II, I, III, V   B. V, I, III, IV, II   C. III, IV, II, V, I   D. I, II, IV, III, V

5.____

6. I. That tough question may be just one question away from an easy one.
    II. They tend to be arranged sequentially: questions on the first paragraph come before questions on the second paragraph.
    III. In summation, it is important not to forget that there is no penalty for guessing.
    IV. Try *all* questions on the passage.
    V. Remember, the critical reading questions after each passage are not arranged in order of difficulty.
    The CORRECT answer is:
    A. I, III, IV, II, V   B. II, I, V, III, IV   C. III, IV, I, V, II   D. V, II, IV, I, III

6.____

7. I. This time of year clients come to me with one goal in mind: losing weight.
    II. I usually tell them that their goal should be focused on fat loss instead of weight loss.
    III. Converting and burning fat while maintaining or building muscle is an art, which also happens to be my job.
    IV. What I love about this line of work is that *everyone* benefits from healthy eating and supplemental nutrition.
    V. This is because most of us have more stored fat than we prefer, but we do not want to lose muscle in addition to the fat.
    The CORRECT answer is:
    A. V, III, I, II, IV   B. I, IV, V, III, IV   C. II, I, III, IV, V   D. II, V, IV, I, II

7.____

8. I. In Tierra del Fuego, "invasive" describes the beaver perfectly.
    II. What started as a small influx of 50 beavers has since grown to a number over 200,000.
    III. Unlike in North America where the beaver has several natural predators that help to maintain manageable population numbers, Tierra del Fuego has no such luxury.
    IV. An invasive species is a non-indigenous animal, fungus, or plant species introduced to an area that has the potential to inflict harm upon the native ecosystem.
    V. It was first introduced in 1946 by the Argentine government in an effort to catalyze a fur trading industry in the region.
    The CORRECT answer is:
    A. IV, I, V, II, III   B. I, IV, II, III, V   C. II, V, III, I, IV   D. V, II, IV, III, I

9. I. The words ensure that we are all part of something much larger than the here and now.
    II. Literature might be thought of as the creative measure of history.
    III. It seems impossible to disconnect most literary works from their historical context.
    IV. Great writers, poets, and playwrights mold their sense of life and the events of their time into works of art.
    V. However, the themes that make their work universal and enduring perhaps do transcend time.
    The CORRECT answer is:
    A. I, III, II, V, IV   B. IV, I, V, II, III   C. II, IV, III, V, I   D. III, V, I, IV, II

10. I. If you don't already have an exercise routine, try to build up to a good 20- to 45-minute aerobic workout.
    II. When your brain is well oxygenated, it works more efficiently, so you do your work better and faster.
    III. Your routine will help you enormously when you sit down to work on homework or even on the day of a test.
    IV. Twenty minutes of cardiovascular exercise is a great warm-up before you start your homework.
    V. Exercise does not just help your muscles; it also helps your brain.
    The CORRECT answer is:
    A. I, IV, II, IV, III   B. IV, V, II, I, III   C. V, III, IV, II, I   D. III, IV, I, V, II

11. I. Experts often suggest that crime resembles an epidemic, but what kind?
    II. If it travels along major transportation routes, the cause is microbial.
    III. Economics professor Karl Smith has a good rule of thumb for categorizing epidemics: if it is along the lines of communication, he says the cause is information.
    IV. However, if it spreads everywhere all at once, the cause is a molecule.
    V. If it spreads out like a fan, the cause is an insect.
    The CORRECT answer is:
    A. I, III, II, V, IV   B. II, I, V, IV, III   C. V, III, I, II, IV   D. IV, V, I, III, II

12.
   I. A recent study had also suggested a link between childhood lead exposure and juvenile delinquency later on.
   II. These ideas all caused Nevin to look into other sources of lead-based items as well, such as gasoline.
   III. In 1994, Rick Nevin was a consultant working for the U.S Department of Housing and Urban Development on the costs and benefits of removing lead paint from old houses.
   IV. Maybe reducing lead exposure could have an effect on violent crime too?
   V. A growing body of research had linked lead exposure in small children with a whole raft of complications later in life, including lower IQ and behavioral problems.
   The CORRECT answer is:
   A. I, III, V, II, IV   B. IV, I, II, V, III   C. I, III, V, IV, II   D. III, V, I, IV, II

12._____

13.
   I. Like Lord Byron a century earlier, he had learn to play himself, his own best hero, with superb conviction.
   II. Or maybe he was Tarzan Hemingway, crouching in the African bush with elephant gun at the ready.
   III. He was Hemingway of the rugged outdoor grin and the hairy chest posing beside the lion he had just shot.
   IV. But even without the legend, the chest-beating, wisecracking pose that was later to seem so absurd, his impact upon us was tremendous.
   V. By the time we were old enough to read Hemingway, he had become legendary.
   The CORRECT answer is:
   A. I, V, II, IV, III   B. II, I, III, IV, V   C. IV, II, V, III, I   D. V, I, III, II, IV

13._____

14.
   I. Why do the electrons that inhabit atoms jump around so strangely, from one bizarrely shaped orbital to another?
   II. And most importantly, why do protons, the bits that give atoms their heft and personality, stick together at all?
   III. Why are some atoms, like sodium, so hyperactive while others, like helium, are so aloof?
   IV. As any good contractor will tell you, a sound structure requires stable materials.
   V. But atoms, the building blocks of everything we know and love—brownies and butterflies and beyond—do not appear to be models of stability.
   The CORRECT answer is:
   A. IV, V, III, I, II   B. V, III, I, II, IV   C. I, IV, II, V, III   D. III, I, IV, II, V

14._____

15.
   I. Current atomic theory suggests that the strong nuclear force is most likely conveyed by massless particles called "gluons".
   II. According to quantum chromodynamics (QCD), protons and neutrons are composed of smaller particles called quarks, which are held together by the gluons.
   III. As a quantum theory, it conceives of space and time as tiny chunks that occasionally misbehave, rather than smooth predictable quantities.

15._____

IV. If you are hoping that QCD ties up atomic behavior with a tidy little bow, you will be disappointed.
V. This quark-binding force has "residue" that extends beyond protons and neutrons themselves to provide enough force to bind the protons and neutrons together.
The CORRECT answer is:
A. III, IV, II, V, I   B. II, I, IV, III, V   C. I, II, V, IV, III   D. V, III, I, IV, II

16. I. I have seen him whip a woman, causing the blood to run half an hour at a time.
II. Mr. Severe, the overseer, used to stand by the door of the quarter, armed with a large hickory stick, ready to whip anyone who was not ready to start at the sound of the horn.
III. This was in the midst of her crying children, pleading for their mother's release.
IV. He seemed to take pleasure in manifesting his fiendish barbarity.
V. Mr. Severe was rightly named: he was a cruel man.
The CORRECT answer is:
A. I, IV, III, II, I   B. II, V, I, III, IV   C. II, V, III, I, IV   D. IV, III, I, V, II

17. I. His death was recorded by the slaves as the result of a merciful providence.
II. His career was cut short.
III. He died very soon after I went to Colonel Lloyd's; and he died as he lived, uttering bitter curses and horrid oaths.
IV. Mr. Severe's place was filled by a Mr. Hopkins.
V. From the rising till the going down of the sun, he was cursing, raving, cutting, and slashing among the slaves in the field.
The CORRECT answer is:
A. V, II, III, I, IV   B. IV, I, III, II, V   C. III, I, IV, V, II   D. I, II, V, III, IV

18. I. The primary reef-building organisms are invertebrate animals known as corals.
II. They are located in warm, shallow, tropical marine waters with enough light to stimulate the growth of reef organisms.
III. Coral reefs are highly diverse ecosystems, supporting greater numbers of fish species than any other marine ecosystem.
IV. They belong to the class Anthozoa and are subdivided into stony corals, which have six tentacles.
V. These corals are small colonial, marine invertebrates.
The CORRECT answer is:
A. I, IV, V, II, III   B. V, I, III, IV, II   C. III, II, I, V, IV   D. IV, V, II, III, I

19. I. Jane Goodall, an English ethologist, is famous for her studies of the chimpanzees of the Gombe Stream Reserve in Tanzania.
II. As a result of her studies, Goodall concluded that chimpanzees are an advanced species closely related to humans.
III. Ultimately, Goodall's observations led her to write *The Chimpanzee Family Book*, which conveys a new, more humane view of wildlife.

IV. She is credited with the first recorded observation of chimps eating meat and using and making tools.
V. Her observations have forced scientists to redefine the characteristics once considered as solely human traits.
The CORRECT answer is:
A. V, II, IV, III, I   B. I, IV, II, V, III   C. I, II, V, IV, III   D. III, V, II, I, IV

20. I. Since then, research has demonstrated that the deposition of atmospheric chemicals is causing widespread acidification of lakes, streams, and soil.
II. "Acid rain" is a popularly used phrase that refers to the deposition of acidifying substances from the atmosphere.
III. This phenomenon became a prominent issue around 1970.
IV. Of the many chemicals that are deposited from the atmosphere, the most important in terms of causing acidity in soil and surface waters are dilute solutions of sulfuric and nitric acids.
V. These chemicals are deposited as acidic rain or snow and include sulfur dioxide, oxides of nitrogen, and tiny particulates such as ammonium sulfate.
The CORRECT answer is:
A. III, IV, I, II, V   B. IV, III, I, IV, V   C. V, I, IV, III, II   D. II, III, I, IV, V

21. I. Programmers wrote algorithmic software that precisely specified both the problem and how to solve it.
II. AI programmers, in contrast, have sought to program computers with flexible rules for seeking solutions to problems.
III. In the 1940 and 1950s, the first large, electronic, digital computers were designed to perform numerical calculations set up by a human programmer.
IV. The computers did so by completing a series of clearly defined steps, or algorithms.
V. An AI program may be designed to modify the rules it is given or to develop entirely new rules.
The CORRECT answer is:
A. I, III, II, V, IV   B. IV, I, III, V, II   C. III, IV, I, II, V   D. III, I, II, IV, V

22. I. Wildfire is a periodic ecological disturbance, associated with the rapid combustion of much of the biomass of an ecosystem.
II. Wildfires themselves are both routine and ecologically necessary.
III. It is where they encounter human habitation, of course, that dangers quickly escalate,
IV. Once ignited by lightning or by humans, the biomass oxidizes as an uncontrolled blaze.
V. This unfettered burning continues until the fire either runs out of fuel or is quenched.
The CORRECT answer is:
A. V, IV, I, II, III   B. I, II, V, III, IV   C. III, II, I, IV, V   D. IV, V, III, I, II

23. I. His arguments supported the positions advanced by the Democratic Party's southern wing and sharply challenged the constitutionality of the Republican Party's emerging political platform.
    II. Beginning in the mid-1840s as a simple freedom suit, the case ended with the Court's intervention in the central political issues of the 1850s and the intensification of the sectional crisis that ultimately led to civil war.
    III. During the Civil War, the decision quickly fell into disrepute, and its major rulings were overruled by ratification of the 13th and 14th Amendments.
    IV. *Dred Scott v. Sandford* ranks as one of the worst decisions in the Supreme Court's history.
    V. Chief Justice Roger Taney, speaking for a deeply divided Court, brought about this turn of events by ruling that no black American—whether free or enslaved—could be a U.S. citizen and that Congress possessed no legitimate authority to prohibit slavery's expansion into the federal territories.
    The CORRECT answer is:
    A. II, IV, I, III, V   B. V, I, III, IV, II   C. I, V, II, V, III   D. IV, II, V, I, III

24. I. Considered the last battle between the U.S. Army and American Indians, the Wounded Knee Massacre took place on the morning of 29 December 1890 beside Wounded Knee Creek on South Dakota's Pine Ridge Reservation.
    II. This was the culmination of the Ghost Dance religion that had started with a Paiute prophet from Nevada named Wovoka (1856-1932), who was also known as Jack Wilson.
    III. During the previous year, U.S. government officials had reduced Sioux lands and cut back rations so severely that the Sioux people were starving.
    IV. These conditions encouraged the desperate embrace of the Ghost Dance.
    V. This pan-tribal ritual had historical antecedents that go much further back than its actual founder.
    The CORRECT answer is:
    A. I, II, III, IV, V   B. V, IV, II, III, I   C. IV, III, I, V, II   D. III, I, V, II, IV

25. I. Their actions, which became known as the Boston Tea Party, set in motion events that led directly to the American Revolution.
    II. Urged on by a crowd of cheering townspeople, the disguised Bostonians destroyed 342 chests of tea estimated to be worth between $10,000 an $18,000.
    III. The Americans, who numbered around 70, shared a common aim: to destroy the ships' cargo of British East India Company tea.
    IV. Many years later, George Hewes, a 31-year-old shoemaker and participant, recalled "We then were ordered by our commander to open the hatches and take out all the chests of tea and throw them overboard. And we immediately proceeded to execute his orders, first cutting and splitting the chests with our tomahawks, so as thoroughly to expose them to the effects of the water.

V. At nine o'clock on the night of December 16, 1773, a band of Bostonians disguised as Native Americans boarded the British merchant ship Dartmouth and two companion vessels anchored at Griffin's Wharf in Boston harbor.

The CORRECT answer is:

A. V, III, IV, II, I   B. IV, II, III, I, V   C. III, IV, V, II, I   D. V, II, IV, III, I

KEY (CORRECT ANSWERS)

1.	A	11.	A
2.	C	12.	D
3.	D	13.	D
4.	B	14.	A
5.	C	15.	C
6.	D	16.	B
7.	B	17.	A
8.	A	18.	C
9.	C	19.	B
10.	B	20.	D

21.	C
22.	B
23.	D
24.	A
25.	A

TEST 2

DIRECTIONS: The sentences listed below are part of a meaningful paragraph, but they are not given in their proper order. You are to decide what would be the BEST order to put sentences to form a well-organized paragraph. Each sentence has a place in the paragraph; there are no extra sentences. *PRINT THE LETTER OF THE CORRECT ANSWER IN THE SPACE AT THE RIGHT.*

1. I. Recently, some U.S. cities have added a new category: compost, organic matter such as food scraps and yard debris.
    II. For example, paper may go in one container, glass and aluminum in another, regular garbage in a third.
    III. Like paper or glass recycling, compositing demands a certain amount of effort from the public in order to be successful.
    IV. Over the past generation, people in many parts of the United States have become accustomed to dividing their household waste products into different categories for recycling.
    V. But the inconveniences of composting are far outweighed by its benefits.
    The CORRECT answer is:
    A. V, II, III, IV, I   B. I, III, IV, V, II   C. IV, II, I, III, V   D. III, I, V, II, IV

    1.____

2. I. It also enhances soil texture, encouraging healthy roots and minimizing the need for chemical fertilizers.
    II. Most people think of banana peels, eggshells, and dead leaves as "waste," but compost is actually a valuable resource with multiple practical uses.
    III. When utilized as a garden fertilizer, compost provides nutrients to soil and improves plant growth while deterring or killing pests and preventing some plant diseases.
    IV. In large quantities, compost can be converted into a natural gas that can be used as fuel for transportation or heating and cooling systems.
    V. Better than soil at holding moisture, compost minimizes water waste and storm runoff, increases savings on watering costs, and helps reduce erosion on embankments near bodies of water.
    The CORRECT answer is:
    A. II, III, I, V, IV   B. I, IV, V, III, II   C. V, II, IV, I,III   D. III, V, II, IV, I

    2.____

3. I. The street is a sea of red, the traditional Chinese color of luck and happiness.
    II. Buildings are draped with festive, red banners and garlands.
    III. Crowds gather then to celebrate Lunar New Year.
    IV. Lamp posts are strung with crimson paper lanterns, which bob in the crisp winter breeze.
    V. At the beginning of February, thousands of people line H Street, the heart of Chinatown in Washington, D.C.
    The CORRECT answer is:
    A. I, V, II, III, IV   B. IV, II, V, I, III   C. III, I, II, IV, V   D. V, III, I, II, IV

    3.____

4. I. Experts agree that the lion dance originated in the Han dynasty; however, there is little agreement about the dance's original purpose.
    II. Another theory is that an emperor, upon waking from a dream about a lion, hired an artist to choreograph the dance.
    III. Dancers must be synchronized with the music accompanying the dance, as well as with each other, in order to fully realize the celebration.
    IV. Whatever the origins are, the current function of the dance is celebration.
    V. Some evidence suggests that the earliest version of the dance was an attempt to ward off an evil spirt.
    The CORRECT answer is:
    A. V, II, IV, III, I   B. I, V, II, IV, III   C. II, I, III, V, IV   D. IV, III, V, I, II

4._____

5. I. Half the population of New York, Toronto, and London do not own cars; instead they use public transport.
    II. Every day, subway systems carry 155 million passengers, thirty-four times the number carried by all the world's airplanes.
    III. Though there are 600 million cars on the planet, and counting, there are also seven billion people, which means most of us get around taking other modes of transportation.
    IV. All of that is to say that even a century and a half after the invention of the internal combustion engine, private car ownership is still an anomaly.
    V. In other words, traveling to work, school, or the market means being a straphanger: someone who relies on public transport.
    The CORRECT answer is:
    A. I, II, IV, V, III   B. III, V, I, II, IV   C. III, I, II, IV, V   D. II, IV, V, III, I

5._____

6. I. "They jumped up like popcorn," he said, describing how they would flap their half-formed wings and take short hops into the air.
    II. Dan settled on the Chukar Partridge as a model species, but he might not have made his discovery without the help of a local rancher that supplied him with the birds.
    III. At field sites around the world, Dan Kiel saw a pattern in how young ground birds ran along behind their parents.
    IV. So when a group of graduate students challenged him to come up with new data on the age-old ground-up-tree-down debate, he designed a project to see what clues might lie in how baby game birds learned to fly.
    V. When the rancher stopped by to see how things were progressing, he yelled at Dan to give the birds something to climb on.
    The CORRECT answer is:
    A. IV, II, V, I, III   B. III, II, I, V, IV   C. III, I, IV, II, V   D. I, II, IV, V, III

6._____

7. I. Honey bees are hosts to the pathogenic large ectoparasitic mite, *Varroa destructor*.
    II. These mites feed on bee hemolymph (blood) and can kill bees directly or by increasing their susceptibility to secondary infections.
    III. Little is known about the natural defenses that keep the mite infections under control.

7._____

IV. Pyrethrums are a group of flowering plants that produce potent insecticides with anti-mite activity.
V. In fact, the human mite infestation known as scabies is treated with a topical pyrethrum cream.
The CORRECT answer is:
A. I, II, III, IV, V   B. V, IV, II, I, III   C. III, IV, V, I, II   D. II, IV, I, III, V

8. I. He hardly ever allowed me to pay for the books he placed in my hands, but when he wasn't looking I'd leave the coins I'd managed to collect on the counter.
    II. My favorite place in the whole city was the Sempere & Sons bookshop on Calle Santa Ana.
    III. It smelled of old paper and dust and it was my sanctuary, my refuge.
    IV. The bookseller would let me sit on a chair in a corner and read any book I liked to my heart's content.
    V. It was only small change—if I'd had to buy a book with that pittance, I would probably have been able to afford only a booklet of cigarette papers.
    The CORRECT answer is:
    A. I, III, V, II, IV   B. II, IV, I, III, V   C. V, I, III, IV, II   D. II, III, IV, I, V

9. I. At school, I had learned to read and write long before the other children.
    II. My father, however, did not see things the way I did; he did not like to see books in the house.
    III. Where my school friends saw notches of ink on incomprehensible pages, I saw light, streets, and people.
    IV. Back then my only friends were made of paper and ink.
    V. Words and the mystery of their hidden science fascinated me, and I saw in them a key with which I could unlock a boundless world.
    The CORRECT answer is:
    A. IV, I, III, V, II   B. I, V, III, IV, II   C. II, I, V, III, IV   D. V, IV, II, III, I

10. I. Gary King of Harvard University says that one main reason null results are not published is because there were many ways to produce them by messing up.
    II. Oddly enough, there is little hard data on how often or why null results are squelched.
    III. The various errors make the null reports almost impossible to predict, Mr. King believes.
    IV. In recent years, the debate has spread to social and behavioral science, which help sway public and social policy.
    V. The question of what to do with null results in research has long been hotly debated among those conducting medical trials.
    The CORRECT answer is:
    A. I, III, IV, V, II   B. V, I, II, IV, III   C. III, II, I, V, IV   D. V, IV, II, I, III

4 (#2)

11.
   I. In a recent study, Stanford political economist Neil Malholtra and two of his graduate students examined all studies funded by TESS (Time-sharing Experiments for Social Sciences).
   II. Scientists of these experiments cited deeper problems within their studies but also believed many journalists wouldn't be interested in their findings.
   III. TESS allows scientists to order up internet-based surveys of a representative sample of U.S. adults to test a particular hypothesis.
   IV. One scientist went on record as saying, "The reality is that null effects do not tell a clear story."
   V. Well, Malholtra's team tracked down working papers from most of the experiments that weren't published to find out what had happened to their results.

   The CORRECT answer is:
   A. IV, II, V, III, I   B. I, III, V, II, IV   C. III, V, I, IV, II   D. I, III, IV, II, V

11.____

12.
   I. The work also suggests that these ultra-tiny salt wires may already exist in sea spray and large underground salt deposits.
   II. Scientists expect for metals such as gold or lead to stretch out at temperatures well below their melting points, but they never expected this superplasticity in a rigid, crystalline material like salt.
   III. Inflexible old salt becomes a softy in the nanoworld, stretching like taffy to more than twice its length, researchers report.
   IV. The findings may lead to new approaches for making nanowires that could end up in solar cells or electronic circuits.
   V. According to Nathan Moore of Sandia National Laboratories, these nanowires are special and much more common than we may think.

   The CORRECT answer is:
   A. IV, III, V, II, I   B. I, V, III, IV, II   C. III, IV, I, V, II   D. V, II, III, I, IV

12.____

13.
   I. The Venus flytrap (Dionaea muscipula) needs to know when an ideal meal is crawling across its leaves.
   II. The large black hairs on their lobes allow the Venus flytraps to literally feel their prey, and they act as triggers that spring the trap closed.
   III. To be clear, if an insect touches just one hair, the trap will not spring shut; but a large enough bug will likely touch two hairs within twenty seconds which is the signal the Venus flytrap waits for.
   IV. Closing its trap requires a huge expense of energy, and reopening can take several hours.
   V. When the proper prey makes its way across the trap, the Dionaea launches into action.

   The CORRECT answer is:
   A. IV, I, V, II, III   B. II, V, I, III, IV   C. I, II, V, IV, III   D. I, IV, II, V, III

13.____

14. I. These books usually contain collections of stories, many of which are much older than the books themselves.
     II. Where other early European authors wrote their literary works in Latin, the Irish began writing down their stories in their own language as early as 6th century B.C.E.
     III. Ireland has the oldest vernacular literature in Europe.
     IV. One of the most famous of these collections is the epic cycle, *The Táin Bó Culainge*, which translates to "The Cattle Raid of Cooley."
     V. While much of the earliest Irish writing has been lost or destroyed, several manuscripts survive from the late medieval period.
     The CORRECT answer is:
     A. V, IV, I, II, III   B. III, II, V, I, IV   C. III, I, IV, V, II   D. IV, II, III, I, V

15. I. Obviously the plot is thin, but it works better as a thematic peace, exploring several great issues that plagued authors and people during that era.
     II. The story begins during a raid when Meb's forces are joined by Frederick and his men.
     III. In the end, many warriors on both sides perish, the prize is lost, and peace is somehow re-established between the opposing sides.
     IV. The middle of the story tells of how Chulu fends off Meb's army by herself while Concho's men struggle against witchcraft.
     V. The prize is defended by the current king, Concho, and the young warrior, Chulu.
     The CORRECT answer is:
     A. II, V, IV, III, I   B. V, I, IV, III, II   C. I, III, V, IV, II   D. III, II, I, V, IV

16. I. However, sometimes the flowers that are treated with the pesticides are not as vibrant as those that did not receive the treatment.
     II. The first phase featured no pesticides and the second featured a pesticide that varied in doses.
     III. In the cultivation of roses, certain pesticides are often applied when the presence of aphids is detected.
     IV. Recently, researchers conducted two phases of an experiment to study the effects of certain pesticides on rose bushes.
     V. To start, aphids are small plant-eating insects known to feed on rose bushes.
     The CORRECT answer is:
     A. IV, III, II, I, V   B. I, II, V, III, IV   C. V, III, I, IV, II   D. II, V, IV, I, III

17. I. My passion for it took hold many years ago when I happened to cross paths with a hiker in a national park.
     II. The wilderness has a way of cleansing the spirit.
     III. His excitement was infectious as he quoted various poetic verses pertaining to the wild; I was hooked.
     IV. For some, backpacking is the ultimate vacation.
     V. While it once felt tedious and tiring, backpacking is now an essential part of my summer recreation.
     The CORRECT answer is:
     A. IV, II, V, I, III   B. II, III, I, IV, V   C. I, IV, II, V, III   D. V, I, III, II, IV

18.
   I. When I was preparing for my two-week vacation to southern Africa, I realized that the continent would be like nothing I have ever seen.
   II. I wanted to explore the continent's urban streets as well as the savannah; it's always been my dream to have "off the grid" experiences as well as touristy ones.
   III. The largest gap in understanding came from an unlikely source; it was the way I played with my host family's dog.
   IV. Upon my arrival to Africa, the people I met welcomed me with open arms.
   V. Aside from the pleasant welcome, it was obvious that our cultural differences were stark, which led to plenty of laughter and confusion.
   The CORRECT answer is:
   A. IV, I, II, III, V   B. III, V, IV, II, I   C. I, IV, II, III, V   D. I, II, IV, V, III

19.
   I. There, I signed up for a full-contact, downhill ice-skating race that looked like a bobsled run.
   II. It wasn't until I took a trip to Montreal that I realized how wrong I was.
   III. As an avid skier and inline skater, I figured I had cornered the market on downhill speeds.
   IV. After avoiding hip and body checks, both of which were perfectly legal, I was able to reach a top speed of forty-five miles per hour!
   V. It was Carnaval season, the time when people from across the province flock to the city for two weeks of food, drink and winter sports.
   The CORRECT answer is:
   A. II, I, III, IV, V   B. III, II, V, I, IV   C. IV, V, I, III, II   D. I, IV, II, V, III

20.
   I. It is a spell that sets upon one's soul and a sense of euphoria is felt by all who experience it.
   II. Pictures and postcards of the Caribbean do not lie; the water there shines with every shade of aquamarine, from pastel to emerald.
   III. As I imagine these sights, I recall one trip in particular that neatly captures the allure of the Caribbean.
   IV. The ocean hypnotizes with its glassy vastness.
   V. On that beautiful day, I was incredibly happy to sail with my family and friends.
   The CORRECT answer is:
   A. I, V, IV, III, II   B. V, I, II, IV, III   C. II, IV, I, III, V   D. I, II, IV, III, V

21.
   I. It wasn't until the early 1700s that it began to resemble the masterpiece museum it is today.
   II. The Louvre contains some of the most famous works of art in the history of the world including the *Mona Lisa* and the *Venus de Milo*.
   III. Before it was a world famous museum, The Louvre was a fort built by King Philip sometime around 1200 A.D.
   IV. The Louvre, in Paris, France, is one of the largest museums in the world.
   V. It has almost 275,000 works of art, which are displayed in over 140 exhibition rooms.
   The CORRECT answer is:
   A. V, I, III, IV, II   B. II, IV, I, V, III   C. V, III, I, IV, II   D. IV, V, II, III, I

22. I. It danced on the glossy hair and bright eyes of two girls, who sat together hemming ruffles for a white muslin dress.
     II. The September sun was glinting cheerfully into a pretty bedroom furnished with blue.
     III. These girls were Clover and Elsie Carr, and it was Clover's first evening dress for which they were hemming ruffles.
     IV. The half-finished skirt of the dress lay on the bed, and as each crisp ruffle was completed, the girls added it to the snowy heap, which looked like a drift of transparent clouds.
     V. It was nearly two years since a certain visit made by Johnnie to Inches Mills and more than three since Clover and Katy had returned home from the boarding school at Hillsover.
     The CORRECT answer is:
     A. III, V, IV, I, II   B. II, I, IV, III, V   C. V, II, I, IV, III   D. II, IV, III, I, V

23. I. The "invisible hand" theory is harshly criticized by parties who argue that untampered self-interest is immoral and that charity is the superior vehicle for community improvement.
     II. Standing as a testament to his benevolence, Smith bequeathed much of his wealth to charity.
     III. Second, Smith was not arguing that all self-interest is positive for society; he simply did not agree that it was necessarily bad.
     IV. First, he was not declaring that people should adopt a pattern of overt self-interest, but rather that people already act in such a way.
     V. Some of these people, though, fail to recognize several important aspects of Adam Smith's the Scottish economist who championed this theory, concept.
     The CORRECT answer is:
     A. I, V, IV, III, II   B. III, IV, II, I, V   C. II, III, V, IV, I   D. IV, III, I, V, II

24. I. Though they rarely are awarded for their many accomplishments, composers and performers continue to innovate and represent a substantial reason for classical music's persistent popularity.
     II. It is often the subject of experimentation on the part of composers and performers.
     III. Even more restrictive is the mainstream definition of "classical," which only includes the music of generations past that has seemingly been pushed aside by such contemporary forms of music as jazz, rock, and rap.
     IV. In spite of its waning limelight, however, classical music occupies an enduring niche in Western culture.
     V. Many people take classical music to be the realm of the symphony orchestra or smaller ensembles of orchestral instruments.
     The CORRECT answer is:
     A. IV, I, III, II, V   B. II, IV, V, I, III   C. V, III, IV, II, I   D. I, V, III, IV, II

25. I. The Great Pyramid at Giza is arguably one of the most fascinating and contentious pieces of architecture in the world.
II. Instead of clarifying or expunging older theories about its age, the results of the study left the researchers mystified.
III. In the 1980s, researchers began focusing on studying the mortar from the pyramid, hoping it would reveal important clues about the pyramid's age and construction.
IV. This discovery was controversial because these dates claimed that the structure was built over 400 years earlier than most archaeologists originally believed it had been constructed.
V. Carbon dating revealed that the pyramid had been built between 3100 BCE and 2850 BCE with an average date of 2977 BCE.

The CORRECT answer is:
A. I, III, II, V, IV   B. II, III, IV, V, I   C. V, I, III, IV, II   D. III, IV, V, I, II

25._____

KEY (CORRECT ANSWERS)

1. C
2. A
3. D
4. B
5. B

6. C
7. A
8. D
9. A
10. D

11. B
12. C
13. D
14. B
15. A

16. C
17. A
18. D
19. B
20. C

21. D
22. B
23. A
24. C
25. A

EXAMINATION SECTION
TEST 1

DIRECTIONS: The sentences listed below are part of a meaningful paragraph, but they are not given in their proper order. You are to decide what would be the BEST order to put sentences to form a well-organized paragraph. Each sentence has a place in the paragraph; there are no extra sentences. *PRINT THE LETTER OF THE CORRECT ANSWER IN THE SPACE AT THE RIGHT.*

Questions 1-3.

DIRECTIONS: Questions 1 through 3 are to be answered on the basis of the following passage.

Almost half of the increase in Chicago came from five neighborhoods, including West Garfield Park. He was 12 years old and had just been recruited into a gang by his older brothers and cousin. A decade later, he sits in Cook County jail, held without bail and awaiting trial on three cases, including felony drug charges and possession of a weapon. Violence in Chicago erupted last year, with the city recording 771 murders—a 58% jump from 2015. They point to a $95 million police-training center in West Garfield Park, public-transit improvements on Chicago's south side and efforts to get major corporations such as Whole Foods and Wal-Mart to invest. Chicago city officials say that they are making strategic investments in ailing neighborhoods. Amarley Coggins remembers the first time he dealt heroin, discreetly approaching a car coming off an interstate highway and into West Garfield park, the neighborhood where he grew up on Chicago's west side.

1. When organized correctly, the first sentence of the paragraph begins with 1.____
   A. "Amarley Coggins remembers…"   B. "He was 12 years old…"
   C. "They point to a…"   D. "Violence in Chicago…"

2. After correctly organizing the paragraph, the author wishes to replace a word 2.____
   in the last sentence with its synonym *enterprises*. Which word does the author wish to replace?
   A. murders   B. neighborhoods
   C. corporations   D. improvements

3. If put together correctly, the second to last sentence would end with the words 3.____
   A. "…Chicago's west side."   B. "…in ailing neighborhoods."
   C. "…older brother and cousins."   D. "…and Wal-Mart to invest."

Questions 4-6.

DIRECTIONS: Questions 4 through 6 are to be answered on the basis of the following passage.

Critics argue that driverless vehicles pose too many risks, including cyberattacks, computer malfunctions, relying on algorithms to make ethical decisions, and fewer transportation jobs. Driverless vehicles, also called autonomous vehicles and self-driving vehicles, are vehicles that can operate without human intervention. And algorithms make decisions based on data obtained from sensors and connectivity. Driverless vehicles rely primarily on three technologies: sensors, connectivity, and algorithms. Sensors observe multiple directions simultaneously. Connectivity accesses information on traffic, weather, road hazards, and navigation. Supporters argue that driverless vehicles have many benefits, including fewer traffic accidents and fatalities, more efficient traffic flows, greater mobility for those who cannot drive, and less pollution. Once the realm of science fiction, driverless vehicles could revolutionize automotive travel over the next few decades.

4. When all of the sentences are organized in correct order, the first sentence starts with
   A. "Connectivity accesses information…"
   B. "Critics argue that…"
   C. "Once the realm of…"
   D. "Driverless vehicles, also called…"

4.____

5. If the above paragraph appeared in correct order, which of the following transition words would be MOST appropriate in the beginning of the sentence that starts "Critics argue that…"
   A. Additionally
   B. To begin,
   C. In conclusion,
   D. Conversely,

5.____

6. When the paragraph is properly arranged, it ends with the words
   A. "…over the next few decades."
   B. "…fewer transportation jobs."
   C. "…and less pollution."
   D. "…without human intervention"

6.____

Questions 7-10.

DIRECTIONS: Questions 7 through 10 are to be answered on the basis of the following passage.

This method had some success, but also carried fatal risks. Various people across Europe independently developed vaccination as an alternative during the later years of the eighteenth century, but Edward Jenner (1749-1823) popularized the practice. Vaccination has been called a miracle of modern medicine, but it has a long and controversial history stretching back to the ancient world. In 1803 the Royal Jennerian Institute was founded in England, and vaccination programs initially drew enormous public support. In 429 BCE in Greece, the historian Thucydides (c.460-c.395 BCE) noted that survivors of smallpox did not become reinfected in subsequent epidemics. Variolation as a means of preventing severe smallpox infection became an accepted practice in China in the tenth century CE, and its popularity spread across Asia,

Europe, and to the Americas by the seventeenth century. Variolation required either inhalation of smallpox dust, or putting scabs or parts of the smallpox pustules under the skin. Widespread inoculation against smallpox was purported to have been part of Ayurvedic tradition as far back as at least 1000 BCE, when Indian doctors traveled to households before the rainy season each year.

7. When arranged properly, what does "This method" refer to in the sentence that begins "This method had some success..."? 7.____
   A. Vaccination
   B. Inoculation
   C. Variolation
   D. Hybridization

8. When organized correctly, the paragraph's third sentence should begin 8.____
   A. "In 429 BCE in Greece..."
   B. "Variolation required..."
   C. "In 1803 the..."
   D. "Vaccination has been called..."

9. If put in the correct order, this paragraph should end with the words 9.____
   A. "...under the skin."
   B. "...to the ancient world."
   C. "...enormous public support."
   D. "...by the seventeenth century."

10. In the second sentence, the author is thinking about using the word immunization instead of which of its synonyms? 10.____
    A. Variolation   B. Vaccination   C. Inhalation   D. Inoculation

Questions 11-13.

DIRECTIONS: Questions 11 through 13 are to be answered on the basis of the following passage.

Summers are hot—often north of 100 degrees—and because it lies at the far end of a San Diego Gas & Electric transmission line, the town has suffered frequent power outages. Another way is that microgrids can ease the entry of intermittent renewable energy sources, like wind and solar, into the modern grid. Utilities are also interested in microgrids because of the money they can save by deferring the need to build new transmission lines. "If you're on the very end of a utility line, everything that happens, happens 10 times worse for you," says Mike Gravely, team leader for energy systems integration at the California Energy Commission. The town has a lot of senior citizens, who can be frail in the heat. Borrego Springs, California, is a quaint town of about 3,400 people set against the Anza-Borrego Desert about 90 miles east of San Diego. High winds, lightning strikes, forest fires and flash floods can bust up that line and kill the electricity. But today, Borrego Springs has a failsafe against power outages: a microgrid. Resiliency is one of the main reasons the market in microgrids is booming, with installed capacity in the United States projected to be more than double between 2017 and 2022, according to a new report on microgrids from GTM Research. "Without air conditioning," says Linda Haddock, head of the local Chamber of Commerce, "people will die."

11. When the sentences above are organized correctly, the paragraph should start with the sentence that begins 11.____
    A. "Borrego Springs, California..."
    B. "But today, Borrego Springs..."
    C. "Summers are hot..."
    D. "Utilities are also interested..."

12. If the author wanted to split this paragraph into two smaller paragraphs, the first sentence of the second paragraph would start with the words
    A. "High winds, lightning strikes, forest fires…"
    B. "But today, Borrego Springs…"
    C. "Resiliency is one of the main…"
    D. "If you're on the very end…"

    12.____

13. Assuming the paragraph were organized correctly, the second to last sentence would end
    A. "…to build new transmission lines."
    B. "…be frail in the heat."
    C. "…into the modern grid."
    D. "…east of San Diego."

    13.____

Questions 14-17.

DIRECTIONS: Questions 14 through 17 are to be answered on the basis of the following passage.

Exhaustive search is not typically a successful approach to problem solving because most interesting problems have search spaces that are simply too large to be dealt with in this manner, even by the fastest computers. Thus, in order to ignore a portion of a search space, some guiding knowledge or insight must exist so that the solution will not be overlooked. This partial understanding is reflected in the fact that a rigid algorithmic solution—a routine and predetermined number of computational steps—cannot be applied. A large part of the intelligence of chess players resides in the heuristics they employ. When search is used to explore the entire solution space, it is said to be exhaustive. Chess is a classic example where humans routinely employ sophisticated heuristics in a search space. Therefore, if one hopes to find a solution (or a reasonably good approximation of a solution) to such a problem, one must selectively explore the problem's search space. Rather, the concept of search is used to solve such problems. Heuristics is a major area of AI that concerns itself with how to limit effectively the exploration of a search space. Many problems that humans are confronted with are not fully understood. The difficulty here is that if part of the search space is not explored, one runs the risk that the solution one seeks will be missed. A chess player will typically search through a small number of possible moves before selecting a move to play. Not every possible move and countermove sequence is explored. Only reasonable sequences are examined.

14. When correctly organized, the paragraph above should begin with the words
    A. "Many problems that…"
    B. "Therefore, if one hopes to…"
    C. "Only reasonable sequences are…"
    D. "The difficulty here is…"

    14.____

15. If the paragraph was organized correctly, the fourth sentence would begin with the words
    A. "Chess is a classic…"   B. "Heuristics is a major…"
    C. "Exhaustive search is not…"   D. "The difficulty here is…"

    15.____

16. If the author wished to separate this paragraph into two equally sized paragraphs, the sentence that begins the second paragraph would END with the words   16._____
    A. "...heuristics they employ."   B. "...in a search space."
    C. "...are not fully employed."   D. "...will be missed."

17. When organized correctly, the paragraph would end with the words   17._____
    A. "...the heuristics they employ."   B. "...will not be overlooked."
    C. "...said to be exhaustive."   D. "...are not fully understood."

Questions 18-21.

DIRECTIONS: Questions 18 through 21 are to be answered on the basis of the following passage.

Asian-Americans soon found themselves the targets of ridicule and attacks. Prior to the bombing he had tried to enlist in the military but was turned down due to poor health. His case, Korematsu v. The United States, is still considered a blemish on the record of the Supreme Court and has received heightened scrutiny given the indefinite confinement of many prisoners after the terrorist attacks on September 11, 2001. On February 19, 1942, President Franklin D. Roosevelt issued Executive Order 9066, which granted the leaders of the armed forces permission to create Military Areas and authorizing the removal of any and all persons from those areas. Fred Korematsu was a 22-year-old welder when the Japanese bombed Pearl Harbor on December 7, 1941. A Nisei—which means an American citizen born to Japanese parents—he was one of four brothers and grew up working in his parents' plant nursery in Oakland, California. This statement effectively pronounced Japanese-Americans on the West Coast as traitors because even though Executive Order 9066 allowed the military to remove any person from designated areas, only those of Japanese descent were ordered to leave. Before Pearl Harbor, he was employed by a defense contractor in California. At the time of the attack, he was having a picnic with his Italian-American girlfriend. Asian-American Fred Korematsu (1919-2005) is most remembered for challenging the legality of Japanese internment during World War II. It was for this simple reason that he eventually became known as a civil rights leader. American reaction to an attack on United States' soil was both swift and harsh. Awarded the Presidential Medal of Honor, he is considered a leader of the civil rights movement in the United States. Roosevelt justified these actions in the opening paragraph of the order by declaring, "the successful prosecution of the war requires every possible protection against espionage, and against sabotage to national-defense material, national-defenses premises and national-defense utilities." Years later he told the San Francisco Chronicle, "I was just living my life, and that's what I wanted to do."

18. When put together correctly, the above paragraph would begin with the words   18._____
    A. "It was for this simple reason..."
    B. "A Nisei—which means..."
    C. "Awarded the Presidential Medal of Honor..."
    D. "Asian-American Fred Korematsu..."

19. If the author wished to separate this piece into two separate paragraphs, the sentence that would be the BEST way to start the second paragraph would begin with the words
    A. "Awarded the Presidential Medal of Honor…"
    B. "Fred Korematsu was a…"
    C. "Roosevelt justified these actions…"
    D. "Before Pearl Harbor, he was…"

19.____

20. In the sentence that begins "A Nisei—which means…", who does "he" refer to in the paragraph?
    A. Roosevelt
    B. A sibling of Korematsu
    C. Fred Korematsu
    D. Japanese-Americans on the West Coast

20.____

21. If organized correctly, the fourth sentence should begin with the words
    A. "At the time of the attack…"
    B. "His case, Korematsu v. The United States…"
    C. "Fred Korematsu was a…"
    D. "This statement effectively pronounced…"

21.____

22. When put together correctly, the last sentence of the paragraph should end with the words
    A. "…that's what I wanted to do."   B. "…were ordered to leave."
    C. "…during World War II."   D. "…was both swift and harsh."

22.____

Questions 23-25.

DIRECTIONS: Questions 23 through 25 are to be answered on the basis of the following passage.

Over the past two decades, her personal finances have been eroded by illness, divorce, the cost of raising two children, the housing bust, and the economic downturn. "There are more people attending college, more people taking out loans, and more people taking out a higher dollar amount of loans," says Matthew Ward, associate director of media relations at the New York Fed. Anderson, who is 57, told her complicated story at a recent Senate Aging Committee hearing (she's previously appeared on the CBS Evening News). Some 3 percent of U.S. households that are headed by a senior citizen now hold federal student debt, mostly debt they took on to finance their own educations, according to a new report from the Government Accountability Office (GAO), an independent agency. She hasn't been able to afford payments on her loans for nearly eight years. Rosemary Anderson has a master's degree, a good job at the University of California (Santa Cruz), and student loans that she could be paying off until she's 81. Student debt has risen across every age group over the past decade, according to a Federal Reserve Bank of New York analysis of credit report data… "As the baby boomers continue to move into retirement, the number of older Americans with defaulted loans will only continue to increase," the report warned. She first enrolled in college in her thirties.

23. When organized correctly, the first sentence should begin with the words
    A. "She first enrolled..."
    B. "Anderson, who is 57..."
    C. "Some 3 percent of..."
    D. "Rosemary Anderson has..."

24. If the author wished to split the paragraph into two paragraphs (not necessarily equal in length), the first sentence of the second paragraph would begin with the words
    A. "Some 3 percent of..."
    B. "There are more people..."
    C. "Over the past two decades..."
    D. "She first enrolled..."

25. When put in the correct order, the second to last sentence should end with the words
    A. "...an independent agency."
    B. "...of credit report data."
    C. "...at the New York Fed."
    D. "...in her thirties."

KEY (CORRECT ANSWERS)

1.	A		11.	A
2.	C		12.	B
3.	B		13.	C
4.	D		14.	A
5.	D		15.	C
6.	B		16.	D
7.	C		17.	A
8.	A		18.	D
9.	C		19.	B
10.	D		20.	C

21.	C
22.	B
23.	D
24.	A
25.	B

TEST 2

DIRECTIONS: The sentences listed below are part of a meaningful paragraph, but they are not given in their proper order. You are to decide what would be the BEST order to put sentences to form a well-organized paragraph. Each sentence has a place in the paragraph; there are no extra sentences. *PRINT THE LETTER OF THE CORRECT ANSWER IN THE SPACE AT THE RIGHT.*

Questions 1-3.

DIRECTIONS: Questions 1 through 3 are to be answered on the basis of the following passage.

According to the World Health Organization (WHO), exposure to ambient (outdoor) air pollution causes 3 million premature deaths around the world each year, largely due to heart and lung diseases. Air pollution also contributes to such environmental threats as smog, acid rain, depletion of the ozone layer, and global climate change. The U.S. Environmental Protection Agency (EPA) sets National Ambient Air Quality Standards (NAAQS) for those four pollutants as well as carbon monoxide (CO) and lead. The EPA also regulates 187 toxic air pollutants, such as asbestos, benzene, dioxin, and mercury. Finally, the EPA places limits on emissions of greenhouse gases like carbon dioxide (CO_2) and methane, which contribute to global climate change. The WHO has established Air Quality Guidelines (ACGs) to identify safe levels of exposure to the emission of four harmful air pollutants worldwide: particulate matter (PM), ozone (O_3), nitrogen dioxide (NO_2), and sulfur dioxide (SO_2). Since EPA criteria define the allowable concentrations of these six substances in ambient air throughout the United States, they are known as criteria air pollutants. Air pollution refers to the release into the air of chemicals and other substances, known as pollutants, that are potentially harmful to human health and the environment.

1. When organized correctly, the first sentence of this paragraph should begin 1.____
   A. "Air pollution refers…"
   B. "The EPA also regulates..,"
   C. "The WHO has established…"
   D. "According to the…"

2. When put in the correct order, the fourth sentence should end with the words 2.____
   A. "…to global climate change."
   B. "…as criteria air pollutants."
   C. "…nitrogen dioxide (NO_2), and sulfur dioxide (SO_2)."
   D. "…health and the environment."

3. If put in the most logical order, the paragraph would end with the words 3.____
   A. "…as criteria air pollutants."
   B. "…to global climate change."
   C. "…benzene, dioxin, and mercury."
   D. "…human health and the environment."

2 (#2)

Questions 4-6.

DIRECTIONS: Questions 4 through 6 are to be answered on the basis of the following passage.

Although gentrification has been associated with some positive impacts, such as urban revitalization and lower crime rates, critics charge that it marginalizes racial and ethnic minorities and destroys the character of urban neighborhoods. British sociologist Ruth Glass is credited with coining the term "gentrification" in her 1964 book *London: Aspects of Change*, which described the transformation that occurred when members of the gentry (an elite or privileged social class) took over working-class districts of London. Gentrification is a type of neighborhood change, a broader term that encompasses various physical, demographic, social, and economic processes that affect distinct residential areas. The arrival of wealthier people leads to new economic development and an increase in property values and rent, which often makes housing unaffordable for longtime residents. Gentrification is a transformation process that typically occurs in urban neighborhoods when higher-income people move in and displace lower-income existing residents.

4. When organized in the correct order, the first sentence of the paragraph should begin with the words
   A. "Gentrification is a type of..."
   B. "British sociologist Ruth..."
   C. "The arrival of..."
   D. "Gentrification is a transformation..."

4._____

5. If put together in the correct order, the second to last sentence in the paragraph would end with the words
   A. "...lower-income existing residents."
   B. "...that affect distinct residential areas."
   C. "...character of urban neighborhoods."
   D. "...working-class districts of London."

5._____

6. If the author wished to change the beginning of the final sentence to "in the end." to better signal the finish of the paragraph, which of the following words would the phrase appear in front of?
   A. British
   B. Gentrification
   C. Although
   D. The

6._____

Questions 7-11.

DIRECTIONS: Questions 7 through 11 are to be answered on the basis of the following passage.

The primary signs of ADHD include a persistent pattern of inattention or hyperactivity lasting in duration for six months or longer with an onset before 12 years of age. Children with ADHD often experience peer rejection, neglect, or teasing and family interactions may contain high levels of discord and negative interactions (APA, 2013). Two primary types of the disorder include inattentive and hyperactive/impulsive, with a combined type when both inattention and hyperactivity occur together. Inattentive ADHD is evidenced by executive functioning deficits such as being off task, lacking sustained focus, and being disorganized. Hyperactive ADHD is evidenced by excessive talkativeness and fidgeting, with an inability to control impulses that may result in harm. Attention Deficit Hyperactivity Disorder (ADHD) is a commonly diagnosed childhood behavioral disorder affecting millions of children in the U.S. every year (National Institute of Mental Health [NIMH], 2012), with prevalence rates between 5% and 11% of the population. Other research has examined singular traits such as executive function deficits in the school setting, task performance in the school setting (Berk, 1986), driving and awareness of time. However, researching academic aspects of the school experience does not provide a comprehensive understanding of the systemic effects of ADHD in the school environment. Historically, much research on ADHD has focused on the academic impact of behavioral symptoms such as reading and mathematics. These behaviors are inappropriate for the child's age level and symptoms typically interfere with functioning in multiple environments.

7. If the author put the paragraph into a logical order, the first sentence would begin with the words
    A. "Inattentive ADHD is…"
    B. "Historically, much research…"
    C. "These behaviors are…"
    D. "Attention Deficit Hyperactivity Disorder…"

    7._____

8. When put in the correct order, what does the author mean by "These behaviors" in the sentence that begins "These behaviors are…"?
    A. Inattention or hyperactivity   B. Reading and Mathematics
    C. Peer rejection   D. Sustained focus

    8._____

9. If the author wished to split this paragraph into two paragraphs (not necessarily equal parts), the first sentence of the second paragraph would BEGIN with the words
    A. "Historically, much research…"
    B. "Other research has examined…"
    C. "Two primary types of…"
    D. "Inattentive ADHD is evidenced…"

    9._____

10. When put in the correct order, the third sentence in the paragraph would END with the words
    A. "…an onset before 12 years of age."
    B. "…5% and 11% of the population."
    C. "…such as reading and mathematics."
    D. "…in multiple environments."

    10._____

11. If the above paragraph was organized correctly, its ending words of the last sentence would be
    A. "…sustained focus, and being disorganized."
    B. "…an onset before 12 years of age."
    C. "…in the school environment."
    D. "…inattention and hyperactivity occur together."

    11._____

Questions 12-15.

DIRECTIONS: Questions 12 through 15 are to be answered on the basis of the following passage.

Health care fraud imposes huge costs on society. In prosecutions of fraud, the DOJ employs the resources of its own criminal and civil divisions, as well as those of the U.S. Attorneys' Offices, HHS, and the FBI. The FBI estimates that health care fraud accounts for at least three and possibly up to ten percent of total health care expenditures, or somewhere between $82 billion and $272 billion each year. Providers are also careful to screen hires for excluded persons or entities lest they be subject to civil monetary penalties. Several government agencies are involved in fighting health care fraud. Individual states assist the HHS Office of the Inspector General ("OIG") and Centers for Medicare & Medicaid Services ("CMS") to initiate and pursue investigations of Medicare and Medicaid fraud. In addition, the OIG uses its permissive exclusion authority to exclude individuals and entities convicted of health care related crimes from federally funded health care services in order to induce providers to help track fraud through a voluntary disclosure program. $30 to $98 billion dollars of that (approximately 36%) is fraud against the public health programs Medicare and Medicaid. The Department of Justice ("DOJ") and the Department of Health and Human Services ("HHS") enforce federal health care fraud law and regulations.

12. When put together in a logical order, the second sentence of the paragraph would end with the words
    A. "...in fighting health care fraud."
    B. "...$272 billion each year."
    C. "...voluntary disclosure program."
    D. "...to civil monetary penalties."

13. In order to organize the paragraph correctly, the sentence that begins "In addition, the OIG..." should FOLLOW the sentence that begins with the words
    A. "$30 to $98 billion dollars of that..."
    B. "Health care fraud..."
    C. "Individual states assist..."
    D. "In prosecutions of fraud..."

14. The author wishes to split the paragraph into a smaller introductory paragraph followed by a slightly longer body paragraph. Which of the following sentences would be BEST to start the second paragraph?
    A. "$30 to $98 billion dollars of that (approximately 36%) is fraud against the public health care programs Medicare and Medicaid."
    B. "Several government agencies are involved in fighting health care fraud."
    C. "In prosecutions of fraud, the DOJ employs the resources of its own criminal and civil divisions, as well as those of the U.S. Attorneys' Offices, HHS, and the FBI."
    D. "Health care fraud imposes huge costs on society."

15. If put together correctly, the paragraph should end with the words	15.____
    A. "...Attorneys' Offices, HHS, and the FBI."
    B. "...huge costs on society."
    C. "...fighting health care fraud."
    D. "...of Medicare and Medicaid fraud."

Questions 16-19.

DIRECTIONS: Questions 16 through 19 are to be answered on the basis of the following passage.

President Abraham Lincoln advocated for granting amnesty to former Confederates to heal the country after the devastating war. Adams and his fellow Federalist Party members in Congress used the law to jail more than a dozen of his political rivals. In 1977, President Jimmy Carter lifted the restrictions on draft dodgers, granting them unconditional amnesty. The issue of amnesty again arose shortly after the U.S. Civil War (1861-1865). Some U.S. government officials, including Vice President Andrew Johnson, advocating placing severe punishments on the military and civilian leaders of the secessionist Confederate States of America. A century later, the controversial nature of the Vietnam War (1964-1975), combined with the compulsory draft for military service, compelled many young men of eligible age to violate the law to avoid the draft. When Thomas Jefferson, Adams' Vice President and opponent of the Alien and Sedition Acts, won the 1800 presidential election, he declared amnesty for those found to have violated the law. Other young men who were drafted deserted the army and refused to serve. In May 1865, when serving as president following Lincoln's assassination, Johnson issued the Proclamation of Amnesty and Reconstruction, which granted the rights of voting and holding office to most former Confederates. In 1974, President Gerald Ford granted amnesty to deserters and "draft dodgers" on the condition that they swear allegiance to the United States and engage in two years of community service. In 1798, President John Adams signed the Alien and Sedition Acts, a set of four laws that restricted criticism of the federal government.

16. When put in the correct order, the paragraph would begin with the following words.	16.____
    A. "Some U.S. government..."   B. "In May 1865, when..."
    C. "A century later, the..."   D. "In 1798, President..."

17. If put in logical order, what sentence number would the sentence that begins	17.____
    "President Abraham Lincoln..." be?
    A. One   B. Six   C. Five   D. Two

18. The author wants to split this paragraph into three separate paragraphs. The	18.____
    THIRD paragraph should begin with the words
    A. "The issue of amnesty again..."   B. "In 1798, President..."
    C. "In 1977, President Jimmy..."   D. "A century later, the..."

19. When organized in sequential order, the last sentence of the paragraph	19.____
    would end with the words
    A. "...of his political rivals."   B. "...after the devastating war."
    C. "...them unconditional amnesty."   D. "...of the federal government."

Questions 20-22.

DIRECTIONS: Questions 20 through 22 are to be answered on the basis of the following passage.

Throughout history, militias have played an important role in national defense against foreign invaders or oppressors. In the original American colonies, state militias served to keep order and played an important role in the fight for independence from the British during the American Revolutionary War. Since that time, state-level militias have continued to exist in the United States alongside a national standing army, providing additional reserve defense and emergency assistance when needed. Some countries still rely almost entirely on public militias for civil defense. In Switzerland, for example, all able-bodied males must serve as part of the Swiss military or civilian service for several months starting when they turn 20 years old and remain reserve militia for years after. Similarly, in Israel, all non-Arab citizens over the age of 18 are required to serve in the Israel Defense Forces for at least two years; Israel is unique in that it requires military service from female citizens as well as males.

20. When put into the correct order, the paragraph should begin with the words
    A. "Throughout history, militias…"   B. "Similarly, in Israel…"
    C. "Some countries still rely…"   D. "Since that time, state-level…"

21. The fifth sentence of the paragraph should end with the words
    A. "…against foreign invaders or oppressors."
    B. "…militias for civil defense."
    C. "…reserve militia for years after."
    D. "…citizens as well as males."

22. The last sentence of the paragraph should end with the words
    A. "…militias for civil defense."
    B. "…citizens as well as males."
    C. "…against foreign invaders or oppressors."
    D. "…during the American Revolutionary War."

Questions 23-25.

DIRECTIONS: Questions 23 through 25 are to be answered on the basis of the following passage.

Medicines such as herbal and homeopathic remedies differ radically from those typically prescribed by mainstream physicians. These practices derive from different cultural traditions and scientific premises. As of 2012, the Memorial Sloan-Kettering Cancer Center offered hypnosis and tai chi, which is an ancient Chinese exercise, to help eases the pains associated with conventional cancer treatments. Some medical professionals staunchly dismiss a number of alternative techniques and theories as quackery. The concept of alternative medicine encompasses an extremely wide range of therapeutic modalities, from acupuncture to yoga. As of 2012, nearly 40 percent of Americans use some alternative medicines or therapies, according to the National Institutes of Health's National Center for Complementary and Alternative Medicine. Alternative approaches to health, fitness, disease prevention, and treatment are sometimes referred to as holistic health care or natural medicine. These names suggest some of the philosophical foundations shared by traditions such as homeopathy, naturopathy, traditional Chinese medicine and herbal medicine. A University of Pennsylvania study in 2010 found that more than 70 percent of U.S. cancer centers offered information on complementary therapies. Increasingly, health care providers are encouraging patients to combine alternative and conventional (or allopathic) treatments, a practice known as complementary or integrative medicine. In the contemporary United States, the phrase alternative medicine has come to mean virtually any healing or wellness practice not based within the conventional system of medical doctors, nurses, and hospitals. Some of these alternative treatments include acupuncture to alleviate pain and nausea and yoga to help reduce stress and manage pain. Yet taken as a whole, the alternative sector of the health field is enormously popular and rapidly growing. The Health Services Research Journal reported in 2011 that three out of four U.S. health care workers used complementary or alternative medicine practices themselves. Other studies have shown that more medical professionals are recommending that cancer patients seek alternative treatments to deal with the side effects of conventional treatments, such as chemotherapy, radiation, and surgery.

23. When put in the correct order, the first sentence should begin with the words
    A. "A University of Pennsylvania study…"
    B. "Other studies have shown that…"
    C. "Increasingly, health care providers…"
    D. "In the contemporary United States…"

24. If the author were to split the paragraph into two separate ones, the first sentence of the second paragraph should begin with the words
    A. "Alternative approaches to health…"
    B. "The concept of alternative medicine…"
    C. "As of 2012, nearly 40%…"
    D. "These names suggest some…"

25. When put into the correct logical sequence, the paragraph should end with the words
    A. "…Complementary and Alternative Medicine."
    B. "…system of medical doctors, nurses, and hospitals."
    C. "…associated with conventional cancer treatments."
    D. "…health care or natural medicine."

KEY (CORRECT ANSWERS)

1. A
2. C
3. B
4. D
5. B

6. C
7. D
8. A
9. A
10. D

11. C
12. B
13. C
14. B
15. A

16. D
17. B
18. D
19. C
20. A

21. C
22. B
23. D
24. A
25. C

PREPARING WRITTEN MATERIAL
EXAMINATION SECTION
TEST 1

DIRECTIONS: Each of the sentences in this test may be classified under one of the following four categories:
- A. *Incorrect* because of faulty grammar or sentence structure
- B. *Incorrect* because of faulty punctuation
- C. *Incorrect* because of faulty capitalization
- D. *Correct*

Examine each sentence carefully to determine under which of the above four options it is best classified. Then, in the space at the right, print the capital letter preceding the option which is the BEST of the four suggested above.

(Each incorrect sentence contains but one type of error. Consider a sentence to be correct if it contains none of the types of errors mentioned, even though there may be other correct ways of expressing the same thought.)

1. This fact, together with those brought out at the previous meeting, prove that the schedule is satisfactory to the employees.   1.____

2. Like many employees in scientific fields, the work of bookkeepers and accountants requires accuracy and neatness.   2.____

3. "What can I do for you," the secretary asked as she motioned to the visitor to take a seat.   3.____

4. Our representative, Mr. Charles will call on you next week to determine whether or not your claim has merit.   4.____

5. We expect you to return in the spring; please do not disappoint us.   5.____

6. Any supervisor, who disregards the just complaints of his subordinates, is remiss in the performance of his duty.   6.____

7. Because she took less than an hour for lunch is no reason for permitting her to leave before five o'clock.   7.____

8. "Miss Smith," said the supervisor, "Please arrange a meeting of the staff for two o'clock on Monday."   8.____

9. A private company's vacation and sick leave allowance usually differs considerably from a public agency.   9.____

10. Therefore, in order to increase the efficiency of operations in the department, a report on the recommended changes in procedures was presented to the departmental committee in charge of the program.   10.____

11. We told him to assign the work to whoever was available. 11._____

12. Since John was the most efficient of any other employee in the bureau, he received the highest service rating. 12._____

13. Only those members of the national organization who resided in the middle West attended the conference in Chicago. 13._____

14. The question of whether the office manager has as yet attained, or indeed can ever hope to secure professional status is one which has been discussed for years. 14._____

15. No one knew who to blame for the error which, we later discovered, resulted in a considerable loss of time. 15._____

KEY (CORRECT ANSWERS)

1.	A	6.	B	11.	D
2.	A	7.	A	12.	A
3.	B	8.	C	13.	C
4.	B	9.	A	14.	B
5.	D	10.	D	15.	A

TEST 2

DIRECTIONS: Each of the sentences in this test may be classified under one of the following four categories:
    A. *Incorrect* because of faulty grammar or sentence structure
    B. *Incorrect* because of faulty punctuation
    C. *Incorrect* because of faulty capitalization
    D. *Correct*

1. The National alliance of Businessmen is trying to persuade private businesses to hire youth in the summertime. 1._____

2. The supervisor who is on vacation, is in charge of processing vouchers. 2._____

3. The activity of the committee at its conferences is always stimulating. 3._____

4. After checking the addresses again, the letters went to the mailroom. 4._____

5. The director, as well as the employees, are interested in sharing the dividends. 5._____

KEY (CORRECT ANSWERS)

1. C
2. B
3. D
4. A
5. A

TEST 3

DIRECTIONS: In each of the following groups of sentences, one of the four sentences is faulty in grammar, punctuation, or capitalization. Select the INCORRECT sentence in each case.

1. A. Sailing down the bay was a thrilling experience for me.
   B. He was not consulted about your joining the club.
   C. This story is different than the one I told you yesterday.
   D. There is no doubt about his being the best player.

   1.____

2. A. He maintains there is but one road to world peace.
   B. It is common knowledge that a child sees much he is not supposed to see.
   C. Much of the bitterness might have been avoided if arbitration had been resorted to earlier in the meeting.
   D. The man decided it would be advisable to marry a girl somewhat younger than him.

   2.____

3. A. In this book, the incident I liked least is where the hero tries to put out the forest fire.
   B. Learning a foreign language will undoubtedly give a person a better understanding of his mother tongue.
   C. His actions made us wonder what he planned to do next.
   D. Because of the war, we were unable to travel during the summer vacation.

   3.____

4. A. The class had no sooner become interested in the lesson than the dismissal bell rang.
   B. There is little agreement about the kind of world to be planned at the peace conference.
   C. "Today," said the teacher, "we shall read 'The Wind in the Willows,' I am sure you'll like it.
   D. The terms of the legal settlement of the family quarrel handicapped both sides for many years.

   4.____

5. A. I was so surprised that I was not able to say a word.
   B. She is taller than any other member of the class.
   C. It would be much more preferable if you were never seen in his company.
   D. We had no choice but to excuse her for being late.

   5.____

KEY (CORRECT ANSWERS)

1. C
2. D
3. A
4. C
5. C

TEST 4

DIRECTIONS: In each of the following groups of sentences, one of the four sentences is faulty in grammar, punctuation, or capitalization. Select the INCORRECT sentence in each case.

1. A. Please send me these data at the earliest opportunity.
   B. The loss of their material proved to be a severe handicap.
   C. My principal objection to this plan is that it is impracticable.
   D. The doll had laid in the rain for an hour and was ruined.

   1.____

2. A. The garden scissors, left out all night in the rain, were in a badly rusted condition.
   B. The girls felt bad about the misunderstanding which had arisen
   C. Sitting near the campfire, the old man told John and I about many exciting adventures he had had.
   D. Neither of us is in a position to undertake a task of that magnitude.

   2.____

3. A. The general concluded that one of the three roads would lead to the besieged city.
   B. The children didn't, as a rule, do hardly anything beyond what they were told to do.
   C. The reason the girl gave for her negligence was that she had acted on the spur of the moment.
   D. The daffodils and tulips look beautiful in that blue vase.

   3.____

4. A. If I was ten years older, I should be interested in this work.
   B. Give the prize to whoever has drawn the best picture.
   C. When you have finished reading the book, take it back to the library.
   D. My drawing is as good as or better than yours.

   4.____

5. A. He asked me whether the substance was animal or vegetable.
   B. An apple which is unripe should not be eaten by a child.
   C. That was an insult to me who am your friend.
   D. Some spy must of reported the matter to the enemy.

   5.____

6. A. Limited time makes quoting the entire message impossible.
   B. Who did she say was going?
   C. The girls in your class have dressed more dolls this year than we.
   D. There was such a large amount of books on the floor that I couldn't find a place for my rocking chair.

   6.____

7. A. What with his sleeplessness and his ill health, he was unable to assume any responsibility for the success of the meeting.
   B. If I had been born in February, I should be celebrating my birthday soon.
   C. In order to prevent breakage, she placed a sheet of paper between each of the plates when she packed them.
   D. After the spring shower, the violets smelled very sweet.

   7.____

2 (#4)

8. A. He had laid the book down very reluctantly before the end of the lesson. 8.____
    B. The dog, I am sorry to say, had lain on the bed all night.
    C. The cloth was first lain on a flat surface; then it was pressed with a hot iron.
    D. While we were in Florida, we lay in the sun until we were noticeably tanned.

9. A. If John was in New York during the recent holiday season, I have no doubt 9.____
       he spent most of the time with his parents.
    B. How could he enjoy the television program; the dog was barking and the
       baby was crying.
    C. When the problem was explained to the class, he must have been asleep.
    D. She wished that her new dress were finished so that she could go to the
       party.

10. A. The engine not only furnishes power but light and heat as well. 10.____
    B. You're aware that we've forgotten whose guilt was established, aren't you?
    C. Everybody knows that the woman made many sacrifices for her children.
    D. A man with his dog and gun is a familiar sight in this neighborhood.

KEY (CORRECT ANSWERS)

1. D   6. D
2. C   7. B
3. B   8. C
4. A   9. B
5. D   10. A

TEST 5

DIRECTIONS: Each of Questions 1 through 5 consists of a sentence which may be classified appropriately under one of the following four categories:
- A. *Incorrect* because of faulty grammar
- B. *Incorrect* because of faulty punctuation
- C. *Incorrect* because of faulty spelling
- D. *Correct*

Examine each sentence carefully. Then, print in the space at the right the letter preceding the category which is the BEST of the four suggested above
(Note: Each incorrect sentence contains only one type of error. Consider a sentence correct if it contains no errors, although there may be other correct ways of writing the sentence.)

1. Of the two employees, the one in our office is the most efficient. 1.____

2. No one can apply or even understand, the new rules and regulations. 2.____

3. A large amount of supplies were stored in the empty office. 3.____

4. If an employee is occassionally asked to work overtime, he should do so willingly. 4.____

5. It is true that the new procedures are difficult to use but, we are certain that you will learn them quickly. 5.____

6. The office manager said that he did not know who would be given a large allotment under the new plan. 6.____

7. It was at the supervisor's request that the clerk agreed to postpone his vacation. 7.____

8. We do not believe that it is necessary for both he and the clerk to attend the conference. 8.____

9. All employees, who display perseverance, will be given adequate recognition. 9.____

10. He regrets that some of us employees are dissatisfied with our new assignments. 10.____

11. "Do you think that the raise was merited," asked the supervisor? 11.____

12. The new manual of procedure is a valuable supplament to our rules and regulations. 12.____

13. The typist admitted that she had attempted to pursuade the other employees to assist her in her work. 13.____

2 (#5)

14. The supervisor asked that all amendments to the regulations be handled by you and I.   14._____

15. The custodian seen the boy who broke the window.   15._____

KEY (CORRECT ANSWERS)

1.	A	6.	D	11.	B
2.	B	7.	D	12.	C
3.	A	8.	A	13.	C
4.	C	9.	B	14.	A
5.	B	10.	D	15.	A

PREPARING WRITTEN MATERIALS

EXAMINATION SECTION

TEST 1

DIRECTIONS: Each question consists of a sentence which may be classified appropriately under one of the following four categories:
- A. Incorrect because of faulty grammar or sentence structure.
- B. Incorrect because of faulty punctuation.
- C. Incorrect because of faulty spelling or capitalization.
- D. Correct

Examine each sentence carefully. Then, in the space at the right, print the capital letter preceding the option which is the BEST of the four suggested above. All incorrect sentences contain only one type of error. Consider a sentence correct if it contains none of the types of errors mentioned, although there may be other correct ways of expressing the same thought.

1. The fire apparently started in the storeroom, which is usually locked.   1.____
2. On approaching the victim two bruises were noticed by this officer.   2.____
3. The officer, who was there examined the report with great care.   3.____
4. Each employee in the office had a separate desk.   4.____
5. The suggested procedure is similar to the one now in use.   5.____
6. No one was more pleased with the new procedure than the chauffeur.   6.____
7. He tried to pursuade her to change the procedure.   7.____
8. The total of the expenses charged to petty cash were high.   8.____
9. An understanding between him and I was finally reached.   9.____
10. It was at the supervisor's request that the clerk agreed to postpone his vacation.   10.____
11. We do not believe that it is necessary for both he and the clerk to attend the conference.   11.____
12. All employees, who display perseverance, will be given adequate recognition.   12.____
13. He regrets that some of us employees are dissatisfied with our new assignments.   13.____

14. "Do you think that the raise was merited," asked the supervisor? 14._____

15. The new manual of procedure is a valuable supplament to our rules and regulation. 15._____

16. The typist admitted that she had attempted to pursuade the other employees to assist her in her work. 16._____

17. The supervisor asked that all amendments to the regulations be handled by you and I. 17._____

18. They told both he and I that the prisoner had escaped. 18._____

19. Any superior officer, who, disregards the just complaints of his subordinates, is remiss in the performance of his duty. 19._____

20. Only those members of the national organization who resided in the Middle west attended the conference in Chicago. 20._____

21. We told him to give the investigation assignment to whoever was available. 21._____

22. Please do not disappoint and embarass us by not appearing in court. 22._____

23. Despite the efforts of the Supervising mechanic, the elevator could not be started. 23._____

24. The U.S. Weather Bureau, weather record for the accident date was checked. 24._____

KEY (CORRECT ANSWERS)

1.	D	11.	A
2.	A	12.	B
3.	B	13.	D
4.	D	14.	B
5.	D	15.	C
6.	D	16.	C
7.	C	17.	A
8.	A	18.	A
9.	A	19.	B
10.	D	20.	C

21.	D
22.	C
23.	C
24.	B

TEST 2

DIRECTIONS: Each question consists of a sentence. Some of the sentences contain errors in English grammar or usage, punctuation, spelling, or capitalization. A sentence does not contain an error simply because it could be written in a different manner. Choose answer:
- A. If the sentence contains an error in English grammar or usage.
- B. if the sentence contains an error in punctuation.
- C. If the sentence contains an error in spelling or capitalization
- D. If the sentence does not contain any errors.

1. The severity of the sentence prescribed by contemporary statutes—including both the former and the revised New York Penal Laws—do not depend on what crime was intended by the offender. 1.____

2. It is generally recognized that two defects in the early law of attempt played a part in the birth of burglary: (1) immunity from prosecution for conduct short of the last act before completion of the crime, and (2) the relatively minor penalty imposed for an attempt (it being a common law misdemeanor) vis-à-vis the completed offense. 2.____

3. The first sentence of the statute is applicable to employees who enter their place of employment, invited guests, and all other persons who have an express or implied license or privilege to enter the premises. 3.____

4. Contemporary criminal codes in the United States generally divide burglary into various degrees, differentiating the categories according to place, time and other attendent circumstances. 4.____

5. The assignment was completed in record time but the payroll for it has not yet been prepaid. 5.____

6. The operator, on the other hand, is willing to learn me how to use the mimeograph. 6.____

7. She is the prettiest of the three sisters. 7.____

8. She doesn't know; if the mail has arrived. 8.____

9. The doorknob of the office door is broke. 9.____

10. Although the department's supply of scratch pads and stationery have diminished considerably, the allotment for our division has not been reduced. 10.____

11. You have not told us whom you wish to designate as your secretary. 11.____

12. Upon reading the minutes of the last meeting, the new proposal was taken up for consideration. 12.____

13. Before beginning the discussion, we locked the door as a precautionery measure. 13.____

14. The supervisor remarked, "Only those clerks, who perform routine work, are permitted to take a rest period." 14.____

15. Not only will this duplicating machine make accurate copies, but it will also produce a quantity of work equal to fifteen transcribing typists. 15.____

16. "Mr. Jones," said the supervisor, "we regret our inability to grant you an extention of your leave of absence." 16.____

17. Although the employees find the work monotonous and fatigueing, they rarely complain. 17.____

18. We completed the tabulation of the receipts on time despite the fact that Miss Smith our fastest operator was absent for over a week. 18.____

19. The reaction of the employees who attended the meeting, as well as the reaction of those who did not attend, indicates clearly that the schedule is satisfactory to everyone concerned. 19.____

20. Of the two employees, the one in our office is the most efficient. 20.____

21. No one can apply or even understand, the new rules and regulations. 21.____

22. A large amount of supplies were stored in the empty office. 22.____

23. If an employee is occassionally asked to work overtime, he should do so willingly. 23.____

24. It is true that the new procedures are difficult to use but, we are certain that you will learn them quickly. 24.____

25. The office manager said that he did not know who would be given a large allotment under the new plan. 25.____

KEY (CORRECT ANSWERS)

1. A
2. D
3. D
4. C
5. C

6. A
7. D
8. B
9. A
10. A

11. D
12. A
13. C
14. B
15. A

16. C
17. C
18. B
19. D
20. A

21. B
22. A
23. C
24. B
25. D

TEST 3

DIRECTIONS: Each of the following sentences may be classified MOST appropriately under one of the following categories:
- A. Faulty because of incorrect grammar
- B. Faulty because of incorrect punctuation
- C. Faulty because of incorrect capitalization
- D. Correct

Examine each sentence carefully. Then, in the space at the right, print the capital letter preceding the option which is the BEST of the four suggested above. All incorrect sentence contain but one type of error. Consider a sentence correct if it contains none of the types of errors mentioned, even though there may be other correct ways of expressing the same thought.

1. The desk, as well as the chairs, were moved out of the office.   1.____

2. The clerk whose production was greatest for the month won a day's vacation as first prize.   2.____

3. Upon entering the room, the employees were found hard at work at their desks.   3.____

4. John Smith our new employee always arrives at work on time.   4.____

5. Punish whoever is guilty of stealing the money.   5.____

6. Intelligent and persistent effort lead to success no matter what the job may be.   6.____

7. The secretary asked, "can you call again at three o'clock?"   7.____

8. He told us, that if the report was not accepted at the next meeting, it would have to be rewritten.   8.____

9. He would not have sent the letter if he had known that it would cause so much excitement.   9.____

10. We all looked forward to him coming to visit us.   10.____

11. If you find that you are unable to complete the assignment please notify me as soon as possible.   11.____

12. Every girl in the office went home on time but me; there was still some work for me to finish.   12.____

13. He wanted to know who the letter was addressed to, Mr. Brown or Mr. Smith.   13.____

14. "Mr. Jones, he said, please answer this letter as soon as possible."   14.____

15. The new clerk had an unusual accent inasmuch as he was born and   15._____
    educated in the south.

16. Although he is younger than her, he earns a higher salary.   16._____

17. Neither of the two administrators are going to attend the conference being   17._____
    held in Washington, D.C.

18. Since Miss Smith and Miss Jones have more experience than us, they have   18._____
    been given more responsible duties.

19. Mr. Shaw the supervisor of the stock room maintains an inventory of stationery   19._____
    and office supplies.

20. Inasmuch as this matter affects both you and I, we should take joint action.   20._____

21. Who do you think will be able to perform this highly technical work?   21._____

22. Of the two employees, John is considered the most competent.   22._____

23. He is not coming home on tuesday; we expect him next week.   23._____

24. Stenographers, as well as typists must be able to type rapidly and accurately.   24._____

25. Having been placed in the safe we were sure that the money would not be   25._____
    stolen.

KEY (CORRECT ANSWERS)

1.	A		11.	B
2.	D		12.	D
3.	A		13.	A
4.	B		14.	B
5.	D		15.	C
6.	A		16.	A
7.	C		17.	A
8.	B		18.	A
9.	D		19.	B
10.	A		20.	A

21. D
22. A
23. C
24. B
25. A

TEST 4

DIRECTIONS: Each of the following sentences consist of four sentences lettered A, B, C, and D. One of the sentences in each group contains an error in grammar or punctuation. Indicate the INCORRECT sentence in each group. *PRINT THE LETTER OF THE CORRECT ANSWER IN THE SPACE AT THE RIGHT.*

1.
   A. Give the message to whoever is on duty.
   B. The teacher who's pupil won first prize presented the award.
   C. Between you and me, I don't expect the program to succeed.
   D. His running to catch the bus caused the accident.

   1.____

2.
   A. The process, which was patented only last year is already obsolete.
   B. His interest in science (which continues to the present) led him to convert his basement into a laboratory.
   C. He described the book as "verbose, repetitious, and bombastic".
   D. Our new director will need to possess three qualities: vision, patience, and fortitude.

   2.____

3.
   A. The length of ladder trucks varies considerably.
   B. The probationary fireman reported to the officer to who he was assigned.
   C. The lecturer emphasized the need for we firemen to be punctual.
   D. Neither the officers nor the members of the company knew about the new procedure.

   3.____

4.
   A. Ham and eggs is the specialty of the house.
   B. He is one of the students who are on probation.
   C. Do you think that either one of us have a chance to be nominated for president of the class?
   D. I assume that either he was to be in charge or you were.

   4.____

5.
   A. Its a long road that has no turn.
   B. To run is more tiring than to walk.
   C. We have been assigned three new reports: namely, the statistical summary, the narrative summary, and the budgetary summary.
   D. Had the first payment been made in January, the second would be due in April.

   5.____

6.
   A. Each employer has his own responsibilities.
   B. If a person speaks correctly, they make a good impression.
   C. Every one of the operators has had her vacation.
   D. Has anybody filed his report?

   6.____

7.
   A. The manager, with all his salesmen, was obliged to go.
   B. Who besides them is to sign the agreement?
   C. One report without the others is incomplete.
   D. Several clerks, as well as the proprietor, was injured.

   7.____

8. A. A suspension of these activities is expected.
    B. The machine is economical because first cost and upkeep are low.
    C. A knowledge of stenography and filing are required for this position.
    D. The condition in which the goods were received shows that the packing was not done properly.

    8.____

9. A. There seems to be a great many reasons for disagreement.
    B. It does not seem possible that they could have failed.
    C. Have there always been too few applicants for these positions?
    D. There is no excuse for these errors.

    9.____

10. A. We shall be pleased to answer your question.
    B. Shall we plan the meeting for Saturday?
    C. I will call you promptly at seven.
    D. Can I borrow your book after you have read it?

    10.____

11. A. You are as capable as I.
    B. Everyone is willing to sign but him and me.
    C. As for he and his assistant, I cannot praise them too highly.
    D. Between you and me, I think he will be dismissed.

    11.____

12. A. Our competitors bid above us last week.
    B. The survey which was began last year has not yet been completed.
    C. The operators had shown that they understood their instructions.
    D. We have never ridden over worse roads.

    12.____

13. A. Who did they say was responsible?
    B. Whom did you suspect?
    C. Who do you suppose it was?
    D. Whom do you mean?

    13.____

14. A. Of the two propositions, this is the worse.
    B. Which report do you consider the best—the one in January or the one in July?
    C. I believe this is the most practicable of the many plans submitted.
    D. He is the youngest employee in the organization.

    14.____

15. A. The firm had but three orders last week.
    B. That doesn't really seem possible.
    C. After twenty years scarcely none of the old business remains.
    D. Has he done nothing about it?

    15.____

KEY (CORRECT ANSWERS)

1.	B	6.	B	11.	C
2.	A	7.	D	12.	B
3.	C	8.	C	13.	A
4.	C	9.	A	14.	B
5.	A	10.	D	15.	C

GLOSSARY OF TERMS
UNDER THE WORKERS' COMPENSATION DISABILITY
BENEFITS VOLUNTEER FIREFIGHTERS' BENEFIT LAWS

CONTENTS

	Page
Accident, Notice and Causal Relationship ..... Application For Review	1
Arising out of an in the Course of Employment ..... Average Weekly Wage	2
Binder...... Claim	3
Claim ...... Covered Employer	4
Date Certain ...... Disability Commencing During Unemployment	5
Disability Benefits Law (Del) ...... Employee Contributions	6
Exclusiveness of Workers' Compensation Remedy ....Hearsay Evidence	7
In Line of Duty ...... Jurisdiction	8
Laches Mr-30	9
No Claim Paper ...... Occupational Disease	10
Plan Benefit ...... Referee	11
Reformation of Insurance Policy .....Second Injury Law	12
Self-Insurance ...... Statute of Limitations	13
Statutory Benefits...... Third Party Settlement	15
Uninsured Employers' Fund.....Waiting Period	16

GLOSSARY OF TERMS
UNDER THE WORKERS' COMPENSATION DISABILITY
BENEFITS VOLUNTEER FIREFIGHTERS' BENEFIT LAWS

A

ACCIDENT, NOTICE AND CAUSAL RELATIONSHIP - (W). The finding made by presiding Referee or the Board that the claimant "sustained an accidental injury arising out of and in the course of employment; that he gave timely notice thereof to his employer; and that the disability is causally related to the accidental injury. (Sec. 2, Subd., 7; Sec. 18)

ACCIDENTAL INJURY - (W). A personal injury which is accidental and which arose out of and in the course of employment, and such disease or infection as may naturally and unavoidably result there from. The term implies an unlocked for mishap or untoward event, and should be construed in line with the common sense view of the average man. (Sec. 2, Subd. 7)

ACTUAL REDUCED EARNINGS (ARE) - (W). The difference between the claimant's post-accident earnings and his pre-accident earnings. (Sec. 14)

ADJOURNMENT ASSESSMENT - (A). A $25.00 assessment which the Board may impose in its discretion for each adjourned hearing held at the request of the carrier.

AFFIDAVIT - (A). A written statement under oath or affirmation made or taken before an officer having authority to administer such oath.

AGGREGATE TRUST FUND - (W). An indivisible trust fund established under Section 27 to assure the payment of worker's compensation in claims involving permanent total disability, the loss of major members and fatal injuries. A private carrier is required and a self-insured employer under certain circumstances is permitted to pay the actuarial value of a claimant's future compensation payments in the above type case into the fund, and upon such payment, the carrier and the self-insured employer are discharged from further liability to such claimant for compensation or death benefits. (Section 27).

ANCR - (W). The abbreviation for ACCIDENT, NOTICE AND CAUSAL RELATIONSHIP. See explanation of the Findings under "Accident, Notice and Causal Relationship," above.

APPEAL - (A). The legal action taken by one of the parties in the Appellate Division, Third Department, to reverse or amend a decision or direction made by a Board Panel or the imposition of an assessment made by the Chairman, Worker's Compensation Board, pursuant to Section 52 (5) of the Law. (Sections 23, 224, W.C.L. and Section 46, V.F.B.L.)

APPLICATION FOR REVIEW - (A). A written request to the Worker's Compensation Board for modification or rescission or review of an award or decision of a Referee, specifying the grounds on which it is made. It must be filed within 30 days after notice of the filing of the decision sought to be reviewed, and should be directed to the Worker's Compensation Board. (Sections 23,224, Board Rule 13 W.C.L. and Section 46, V.F.B.L.)

177

ARISING OUT OF AN IN THE COURSE OF EMPLOYMENT - (W). The injury that "arises out of" the employment is one that was caused by a hazard of the employment. The injury that is "in the course of employment" is one that arose at a time, place and under circumstances related to the employment. Both conditions must be satisfied in order to establish a work-connected accidental injury. (Section 2, Subd. 7)

AUTHORIZED PHYSICIAN - (A). A physician licensed to practice medicine in the State of New York who has been authorized by the Chairman of the Workers' Compensation Board to render medical care or treatment under the Workers' Compensation Law. The authorization specifies the character of the medical care which the physician is authorized to render. (Section 13-b, Subd. 2; Reg. 110)

AUTHORIZED PODIATRIST - (A). A podiatrist licensed to practice podiatry in the State of New York who has been authorized by the Chairman of the Workers' Compensation Board to render podiatric care or-treatment under the Workers' Compensation Law. When care is required for injury to the foot, the injured worker may select to treat him any authorized physician or podiatrist. (Section 13-k; Reg. 110)

AUTHORIZED CHIROPRACTOR - (A). A chiropractor licensed to practice chiropractic in the State of New York who has been authorized by the Chairman of the Workers' Compensation Board to render chiropractic care under the Workers' Compensation Law within the limits prescribed by the Education Law.

AVERAGE WEEKLY WAGE - (W). The average weekly wage is one-fifty second part of the average annual earnings of the injured worker. Such average annual earnings are computed in one of the following ways: If the claimant worked in the employment in which he was injured, substantially the whole year preceding the injury, whether for the same employer or not, his average annual earnings will consist of three hundred times his average daily wage if he was a six-day worker, and two-hundred and sixty times his average daily wage if he was a five-day worker. A claimant who has worked ninety percent of the year preceding the injury, is deemed to have worked substantially the whole of the year. In the event the claimant has not worked a substantial part of the year, the average daily wage of another employee of the same class, who has worked substantially the whole of such immediately preceding year in the same or similar employment, in the same or a neighboring area will be used to fix the claimant's average annual earnings. Where the employment itself as distinguished from the claimant's relationship to it, is intermittent or discontinuous, and the multiplication of claimant's average daily wage by either the three-hundred multiple or the two-hundred and sixty multiple will not accurately reflect his annual earning capacity, the claimant's average annual earnings will be fixed at two-hundred times his average daily wage in the employment in which he was injured. (Section 14)

AVERAGE WEEKLY WAGE - (D). The amount determined by dividing the total wages of an employee in the employment of his last covered employer for the eight weeks or portion thereof that the employee was in such employment immediately preceding and including his last day worked prior to the commencement of such disability, by the number of weeks or portion thereof of such employment. (Section 201, Subd. 12)

B

BINDER - (A). A temporary insurance contract which, except for specified differences, contains the terms of the contract which will replace it. The binder obligates the carrier to fulfill the terms of the contract just as if the final contract were in effect.

BOARD OF CONSULTANTS - (W). Two compensation examining physicians appointed by the Board Medical Director to examine a claimant when objection is taken to the report of another compensation examining physician in schedule type cases exclusive of eye and ear cases.

BOARD DENIAL - (A). A Board decision denying the relief sought in an application for review of a Referee decision because the record developed at the Referee hearing(s) supports the Referee decision. (Sections 23, 224)

BOARD PANEL - (A). A panel of three Board Members who render decisions on applications for review of Referee decisions. The decision of a Board Panel is deemed the decision of the Board. (Section 142)

BOARD REVIEW - (A). Where a Referee decision is disputed, the aggrieved party may file an application for a review thereof with the Board. The Board's decision on the application will contain a statement of the facts which formed the basis of its action on the issue raised. Appeals from Board decisions may be taken to the Appellate Division of the Supreme Court, Third Department, and thereafter to the Court of Appeals. (Sections 23, 224, Board Rule 13)

C

CALENDAR - (A). A list of cases scheduled to be heard on a given date at a specific part or hearing point. (Section 141; Board Rules 4, 7, 8, and 9)

CARRIER - (W.V). The term applies to the State Fund, stock corporations, mutual corporations or reciprocal insurers with which employers cover their liability under the Workers' Compensation Law, the Disability Benefits Law and the Volunteer Firefighters' Benefit Law. The term also applies to self-insured employers. The carrier is liable for the payment of benefits and where indicated, medical care. (Section 2, Subd. 12; Section 50, Subd. 3)

CARRIER - (D). The term applies to the State Fund, stock or mutual corporations, and reciprocal insurers which insure the payment of disability benefits; and employers and associations of employers or of employees and trustees authorized or permitted to pay benefits. (Section 201, Subd. 11)

CAUSAL RELATIONSHIP - (W,V). The connection between the claimant's physical condition and his accidental injury or occupational disease. (Section 2, Subd. 7)

CHIROPRACTIC FEE SCHEDULE - (W.V.). The schedule established by the Chairman of the Workers' Compensation Board of changes and fees for chiropractic treatment and care furnished to workers' compensation claimants. (Section 13-1).

CLAIM - (W). A request on a prescribed form C-3 for workers' compensation for work-connected injury, occupational disease disablement, or death (form C-62) resulting from either cause. A claimant must file a claim within a two-year period from the occurrence of the accidental injury, occupational disablement or death. Failure may bar an award for compensation unless the employer has made advance benefit payments in which event the claim filing requirement is deemed waived. (Sections 20, 28)

CLAIM - (D). A request for disability benefits on a prescribed form DB-450, used if the employee becomes sick or disabled (a) while employed, (b) while on a paid leave of absence or paid vacation, or (c) within four weeks after termination of employment. Completed Claim form DB-450 should be mailed to the employer or his disability benefits insurance carrier. Also, a request for disability benefits on a prescribed form DB-300, used by the employee if he becomes sick or disabled after four weeks of unemployment. Completed claim form DB-300 should be mailed to the Chairman, Workers' Compensation Board, Disability Benefits Bureau, 1949 North Broadway, Albany, New York 12204

COMMITTEE - (A). A responsible person or persons appointed by a court to protect the interests of a mental incompetent. If a committee has not been appointed, the time limitations under the Workers' Compensation Law do not run. (Section 115)

COMMUTED AWARD - (W,V). The actuarially determined value of an award, payable biweekly for a period of future disability, which is changed into a single fixed or gross sum payable into the Aggregate Trust Fund or which forms the basis for a payment to a nonresident alien. (Section 15, Subd. 5-b; Sections 17, 25, 25-b, 27, W.C.L. and Sections 17, 54, V.F.B.L.)

COMPENSATION EXAMINING PHYSICIAN - (A). A physician appointed under Civil Service Regulations to examine claimants for the Workers' Compensation Board. (Section 19)

CONSEQUENTIAL ACCIDENT - (W,V). A second accident resulting from a prior accidental injury which arose out of and in the course of employment. For example, a claimant falling down a flight of stairs at home while using crutches because of a leg injury incurred at work. (Section 2, Subd. 7)

CONTINUING JURISDICTION - (A). The jurisdiction of the Workers' Compensation Board over a workers' compensation claim is continuing, and the Board may from time to time within its discretion, reconsider a claim, change its findings, and either make new awards or modify outstanding awards as in its opinion may appear just. (Section 123)

CONTROVERTED CLAIM - (A). A claim rejected by the carrier on stated grounds. A hearing for the determination of these grounds is set by the Board, and the parties are directed to appear and present their case. (Section 25)

COVERED EMPLOYER - (D). An employer of one or more employees on each of at least 30 days in any calendar year becomes a covered-employer from and after the expiration of four weeks following such 30th day. An employer of personal or domestic employees in a private home becomes a covered employer from and after the expiration of four weeks following employment of four such employees on each of at least 30 days in any calendar year. (Section 202)

D

DATE CERTAIN - (A). An action taken by a Referee at a hearing in which he arranges for the next hearing of the case on a particular day and time when required witnesses may appear.

DAY OF DISABILITY - (D). Any day on which the employee was prevented from performing work because of disability and for which he has not received his regular remuneration. (Section 201, Subd. 14)

DEFICIENCY COMPENSATION-(W.V.) The difference between the net recovery in a third party action instituted by a claimant on account of a work-connected accidental injury and the amount of workers' compensation payable for such injury, if such amount is larger. Deficiency compensation is payable by the workers' compensation carrier. (Section 29, W.C.L. and Section 20 V.F.B.L.)

DEPENDENCY - (W,V). Death benefits in a fatal injury case may be payable, under certain circumstances, to surviving blind or crippled dependent children over the age of 18, dependent grandchildren, brothers and sisters under the age of 18, and dependent parents and grandparents. These claimants must prove their dependency upon the deceased employee. The regular receipt of contributions by the alleged dependent upon which he relies and which he needs, even if only partially, to sustain him in his customary mode of living, constitutes dependency. The surviving widow, or children under 18 years of age are not required to prove dependency. (Section 15, Subd. 4; Section 16)

DEPOSITION - (A). Evidence of testimony of a witness based upon a series of questions drawn up for the purpose of ascertaining the facts. Depositions are taken where witnesses cannot appear at a hearing before the Board. The questions and answers are part of a proceeding before an official person. (Section 121; Board Rule 19)

DISABILITY (TOTAL)* - (W,V). Disability, medically established, which precludes a claimant from earning any wages. (Section 15, Subds. 1,2)

DISABILITY (PARTIAL) - (W,V). Disability which allows a claimant to engage in some kind of gainful employment. The difference between the claimant's pre-accident earnings and his post-accident earnings is determinative of his reduced earnings rate. In the absence of actual post-accident earnings, the Board may in the interest of justice fix such wage earning capacity as is reasonable. (Section 15, Subds. 5, 5-a)

DISABILITY COMMENCING DURING EMPLOYMENT - (D). The inability of an employee, as the result of injury or sickness not arising out of and in the course of employment, to perform the regular duties of his employment or the duties of any other employment which his employer may offer him at his regular wages. (Section 201, Subd. 9)

DISABILITY COMMENCING DURING UNEMPLOYMENT - (D). The inability of an employee, as the result of injury or sickness not arising out of and in the course of employment, to perform the duties of any employment for which he is reasonably qualified by training and experience. (Section 201, Subd. 9)

DISABILITY BENEFITS LAW (DEL) - (D). The non-occupational Disability Benefits Law which provides for the payment of benefits to workers out of work because of illness or disabling accidents not connected with their employment.

DOUBLE COMPENSATION - (W). A duplicate award of either compensation or death benefits made on the ground that the injured employee, at the time of the accident, was under the age of 18 years and was permitted or suffered to work in violation of the New York Labor Law or of a rule of the Board of Standards and Appeals. The employer alone and not his carrier is liable for the additional compensation. (Section 14-a)

DOUBLE INDEMNITY - (W). The same as Double Compensation. See explanation appearing immediately above.

E

EARNING CAPACITY - (W). The ability of a claimant, who has suffered a work-connected disabling injury, to earn wages in the labor market. A claimant's earning capacity is determined by his actual post-accident earnings. In the event he has no actual earnings, the Board may establish a theoretic wage earning capacity which is reasonable on the basis of the record but not in excess of 75% of the claimant's former full time actual earnings. (Section 15, Subd. 5-a)

ELECTION OF REMEDIES - (W). The right of a claimant whose employer was uninsured at time of the accident, to bring a court action against such employer in lieu of claiming workers' compensation (Section 11)

EMPLOYEE CONTRIBUTIONS - (D). An employee may be required to contribute 1/2 of 1% of the first $60.00 of his weekly wage, but not more than 30 cents per week. Where benefits are being provided under a plan approved by the Chairman, contributions of employees may be reduced or eliminated; or may be at a higher rate if the employer and employees have agreed thereto and the employee contribution is reasonably related, in the judgment of the Chairman, to the value of the benefits payable. (Section 209, Subd. 3)

EXCLUSIVENESS OF WORKERS' COMPENSATION REMEDY - (W). The legislature has established the Workers' Compensation Law as the exclusive remedy of an employee and his personal representatives against his employer who has secured workers' compensation. It is the sole recourse that the injured employee, his dependents or representatives have against the employer for injuries or death resulting from a work-connected accident or occupational disease. If an employer who is required to secure workers' compensation insurance fails to do so, his employee if disabled due to a work-connected injury, has the right to elect to either claim workers' compensation or to maintain an action against the uninsured employer for damages. (Section 11)

---

*For definition of "disability" under the off-the-job Disability Benefits Law see DAY OF DISABILITY, DISABILITY COMMENCING DURING EMPLOYMENT AND DISABILITY COMMENCING DURING UNEMPLOYMENT.

F

FACIAL DISFIGUREMENT AWARD - (W). An award of compensation for serious permanent facial or head disfigurement.

FINAL ADJUSTMENT (FA) - (W.V). A hearing held in cases involving the loss or loss of use of a member or organ of the body in which the principal issue is the extent of loss or loss of use. (Section 15, Subd. 3)

FUND FOR REOPENED CASES - (W,V). A fund created under the Workers' Compensation Law to assume liability for claims of compensation in certain "stale" cases where specified time limits have elapsed. (Section 25-a, W.C.L. and Section 51, V.F.B.L.)

G

GENERAL EMPLOYER - (W). The general employer is the regular or parent employer who makes his employee available to a special employer. The general employer usually exercises indirect control and the special employer exercises direct control. If the employee is injured, either employer or both may be liable for the compensation due to the injured employee. (Section 2, Subds. 3,4)

H

HEARING - (W.V). The Law provides that "No case shall be closed without notice to all parties interested and without giving to all such parties an opportunity to be heard." These "hearings" are held before Referees who hear and determine claims for compensation for the purpose of ascertaining the substantial rights of the parties. (Sections 20, 150)

HEARING - (D). When an employee files with the Chairman a notice that his claim for disability benefits has not been paid, a hearing is held only if requested by the claimant, carrier or employer, or if the issue cannot be resolved administratively.

HEARSAY EVIDENCE - (A). Testimony based upon second-hand information not known directly by the witness but related to him by someone else, constitutes hearsay evidence. It is admissible in a workmen's compensation proceedings. Declarations of a deceased employee concerning the accident are receivable in evidence, and if corroborated by circumstances or other evidence are sufficient to establish the accident and the injury. (Section 118)

I

IN LINE OF DUTY - (V). Injuries to volunteer firefighters are deemed to be in line of duty if incurred in the course of necessary travel to and from, and work at a fire, alarm of fire or other emergency to which the fire company or any unit thereof has responded, or would be required or authorized to respond and necessary travel during such work. It also covers (1) the performance, pursuant to orders of authorization, including necessary travel directly connected therewith, of duties in the firehouse or elsewhere and the investigation thereof as well as the inspection of property for fire hazards or other dangerous conditions; (2) instruction in fire duties and authorized attendance at a fire school; (3) attendance or work at meetings of the fire department or fire company or any unit thereof; (4) work in connection with the construction, testing, inspection, repair or maintenance of the firehouse and the fixtures, furnishings and equipment thereof, the fire fighting vehicles, fire apparatus and equipment, the fire alarm system, water supply system, fire well, fire cistern or fire suction pool used by the fire department or fire company or other unit thereof; (5) engaging in the inspection of fire fighting vehicles and fire apparatus prior to delivery under a contract of purchase, or performing duties in relation to the delivery thereof; (6) authorized participation in any drill, parade, inspection or review or any competitive tournament, contest or public exhibition in which the fire company or department or any unit thereof is engaged, and attendance at a convention or conference as an authorized delegate of the fire department, company or unit thereof; (7) authorized work in connection with a fund-raising activity of the fire company within the limits of Section 204-a of the General Municipal Law. It also extends to necessary travel to, work in connection with, and necessary travel returning from a call for general ambulance service by a member of an emergency relief squad which has been authorized to furnish such service pursuant to Section 209-b of the General Municipal Law. (Section 3, Subd. 3; Section 5, Volunteer Firefighters' Benefit Law)

INDEXED CLAIM - (W,V). A claim case folder when assembled is referred to as an indexed claim. (Section 141)

INJURY - (D). Injury and sickness mean accidental injury, disease, infection or illness which do not arise out of and in the course of employment. (Section 201, Subd. 8)

J

JURISDICTION - (W). The Workers' Compensation Board has the right to hear and determine a workmen's compensation case if the employment was located in New York. Proof of the latter would be some of the following contacts with New York State: (1) hiring in New York, (2) work in New York, (3) control of out-of-state employment from New York, (4) residency of claimant in New York, (5) understanding that claimant is to return to New York, following completion of the out-of-state assignment, and (6) occurrence of injury in New York.

JURISDICTION - (D). The Workers' Compensation Board has the right to hear and determine a disability benefits case if the employment is localized in New York; i.e., if it is performed entirely within the State or is performed both within and without the State but that performed without the State is incidental to the employment within the State or is temporary or transitory in nature or consists of isolated transactions; or where the employment is not localized in any state, if the employee's base of operations is in New York; or where there is no base of operations in any state, if the place from which the employment is directed or controlled is in New York; or where the base of operations or place from which the employment is controlled or directed is not in any state in which some part of the service is performed, if the employee's residence is in New York. (Section 201, Subd. 6-c)

L

LACHES - (A). The failure by a party to assert a right or request the enforcement of a right for a period of time which is unreasonable and unexplained.

LICENSED REPRESENTATIVE - (A). A person other than an attorney who is authorized by the Workers' Compensation Board to represent claimants before the Board, and in some instances, to receive a fee, fixed by the Board, for such services. Also, a person other than an attorney who is authorized by the Workers' Compensation Board to represent self-insurers before the Board. (Sections 24-a, 50(3-b); 225); Board Rule re Licences)

LOST TIME (LT) - (A). The phrase indicates that the claimant's disability has caused lost time and loss of earnings beyond the waiting period (the first seven days of disability). In workmen's compensation cases only, if the disability exceeds 14 days, compensation will be payable from the first day of disability. There is no waiting period in V.F.B.L. cases. (Sections 12, 204-1)

LUMP-SUM NON-SCHEDULE ADJUSTMENT - (W.V). A lump sum paid to a claimant in a non-schedule disability case in which the continuance of disability and of future earning capacity cannot be ascertained with reasonable certainty. Such lump sums must be submitted to the Board for approval after they have been agreed to by the claimant and the carrier. (Section 15, Subd. 5-b)

M

MEDICAL FEE SCHEDULE - (W,V). The schedule established by the Chairman of the Workers' Compensation Board of charges and fees for medical treatment and care furnished to workmen's compensation claimants. (Section 13, Subd. (a))

MODIFY PREVIOUS AWARD (MPA) - (A). A direction by a presiding Referee or a Board Panel ending, reducing or increasing the workers' compensation previously awarded to the claimant. (Sections 22, 223)

MOTION CALENDAR HEARING - (W,V). A regularly scheduled hearing on a case in which no controversy exists. The notice of hearing contains the proposed decision, and the interested parties are advised that they need not be present at the hearing.

MR-30 - (W,V). Request by Board's Medical Registration Office for decision relative to com-pensability of claim or other issue triable by a Referee, as a prerequisite to taking action on a disputed medical bill. It is instituted following receipt of Form A-1.

N

NO CLAIM PAPER - (W). A form, paper or correspondence receivedby the Board which does not warrant the indexing of a claim case folder. These papers are filed in the No-Claim File.

NO-DEPENDENCY DEATH CASE - (W,V). A death case in which there are no persons eligible to receive workmen's compensation benefits. In such case, the employer or his insurance carrier pays the funeral expenses, not exceeding $750.00 and $1,000 into the Vocational Rehabilitation Fund, and $1,500 into the Special Fund for Reopened Cases. Under certain circumstances, the $1,500 payment is paid to the Uninsured Employers' Fund instead. (Sections 15(9), 16(1) and 25-a(3), W.C.L. and Sections 15, 51, V.F.B.L.)

NO LOST TIME (NLT) - (W). Claimant has not lost time beyond the waiting period (the first seven days of disability) as a result of his work-connected injuries. (Section 12)

NON-INSURER - (W,D). A subject employer who has failed to provide for the payment of benefits to his employees either under the Workers' Compensation Law or under the Disability Benefits Law. (Sections 50, 220)

NOTICE - (W). Employees who are injured on-the-job must give their employers notice in writing of the occurrence as soon as possible but not later than 30 days thereafter. The Board may excuse the failure to give notice on the ground that notice for some sufficient reason could not have been given or on the ground that the employer had knowledge of the accident or on the ground that the employer had not been prejudiced thereby. In addition, a claim must be filed with the Board within two years. Failure to file a claim may bar an award of compensation unless the employer has made advance payments to the injured worker or has failed to raise the issue at the first hearing at which all parties were present. (Sections 18, 28, 40 and 45)

NOTICE AND PROOF OF CLAIM - (D). Employees who are disabled due to an off-the-job injury or illness must furnish written notice of disability to the employer within fifteen days and must furnish proof of disability (completed by the employee's physician or podiatrist or chiropractor) within twenty days. The prescribed notice and proof are the Claim Forms DB-300 and DB-450. Failure to furnish proof of disability within the 20-day period does not invalidate the claim, but no benefits are required to be paid for any period of disability more than two weeks prior to the date on which the proof was furnished, unless it be shown to the satisfaction of the Chairman that it had not been reasonably possible to furnish it within the prescribed time and that it was done as soon as possible. However, no benefits shall be paid unless the proof of disability was furnished within twenty-six weeks after the commencement of disability.

NOTICE - (V). Under the Volunteer Firemen's Benefit Law, notice of injury or death must be given by the injured volunteer fireman or his dependents within 90 days after the injury or death. (See Q. and A. 14 under the Volunteer Firefighters' Benefit Law)

O

OCCUPATIONAL DISEASE - (W,V). A disease arising from the conditions to which all employees of a class are subject and which produces the disease as a natural incident of a particular occupation as distinguished from and exceeding the hazard and risk of ordinary employment. A disease does not become an occupational disease merely because it is contracted on the employer's premises'in the course of the employment; it must be one which is commonly regarded as natural to, inhering in, or an incident of the work in question. There must be a recognizable link between the disease and some distinctive feature of the claimant's job. (Sections 3(2), 37, 49-a)

P

PLAN BENEFIT - (D). Disability Benefits provided under a plan or agreement accepted by the Chairman. An employer, unilaterally or as a result of collective bargaining may provide plan benefits, i.e. benefits that differ from statutory benefits in amounts of benefits paid, duration of benefits and waiting period. Plan benefits may also include hospital, surgical and/or medical care benefits. (Section 211)

PODIATRY FEE SCHEDULE - (W.V). The schedule established by the Chairman of the Workers' Compensation Board of charges and fees for podiatric treatment and care furnished to workers' compensation claimants. (Section 13-K)

PRESUMPTIONS - (W). In a claim for workers' compensation, it is presumed in the absence of substantial evidence to the contrary, that the claim falls within the Law; that sufficient notice was given; that the injury was not occasioned by the willful intention of the injured employee to bring about the injury or death of himself or another; and that death did not result solely from the intoxication of the injured employee. (Sections 21, 47)

PROTRACTED HEALING PERIOD - (W,V). In case of temporary total disability and permanent partial disability both resulting from the same schedule injury, if the period of temporary total disability continues for a longer period than the normal healing period as set forth in Section 15, Subd. 4-a, the period of temporary total disability in excess of such normal healing period is added to the schedule award. (Section 15, Subd. 4-a, W.C.L. and Section 9, V.F.B.L.)

PROOF OF CLAIM - (D). See "Notice and Proof of Claim".

R

RED SEAL SUMMONS - (W,D). A summons issued by the Board requiring an employer to appear at the Board or to furnish information by mail regarding his compliance with either the Workmen's Compensation Law or the Disability Benefits Law.

REDUCED EARNINGS (RE) - (W). A compensation rate based on the claimant's reduced earnings or his reduced earning capacity due to a condition related to his compensable work-connected injury. (Section 15)

REFEREE - (A). A quasi-judicial officer appointed by the Workers' Compensation Board to hear and determine claims and to conduct such hearings and investigations and make such orders, decisions, and determinations as may be required in the adjudication of the claims. His decision is deemed the decision of the Board unless the Board modifies or rescinds such decision. (Section 150)

REFORMATION OF INSURANCE POLICY - (A). The Workers' Compensation Board has the power to reform or rectify an insurance policy whenever the policy fails through fraud or mutual mistake to reflect the real agreement or actual intention of the parties.

REHABILITATION - (W,V). The process of restoring injured workers to productive employment through physical means, medical procedures, vocational retraining, selective placement, and social readjustment. Rehabilitation is an integral part of the medical care and other services furnished a claimant under the Law. (Section 13, Subd. a)

REMARRIAGE AWARD - (W,V). An award of two years' compensation paid in a lump sum, to the surviving widow or surviving dependent widower of a fatally injured worker upon her or his remarriage. (Section 16, Subd. 2)

REOPENED CASE - (A). A case which has been closed by a Referee or the Board, and is subsequently made active again to determine the claimant's eligibility for benefits. (Sections 22, 23 and 224)

REOPENED CASES FUND - (W,V). When an application to reopen a closed case is made more than seven years from the date of injury and more than three years from the date of the last payment of compensation, liability for any additional workers' compensation awarded in the case is imposed against the Reopened Cases Fund. The latter is financed through payments in non-dependency death cases and through assessments made periodically against all carriers. (Section 25-a, W.C.L. and Section 51, V.F.B.L.)

REQUEST FOR REIMBURSEMENT - (A). A request by an employer for reimbursement of wages paid to an employee for a period during which he was eligible to receive workers' compensation or disability benefits. Also, a request by a Compensation carrier for reimbursement out of the Special Disability Fund (Second Injury Fund); and a request by a Disability Benefits carrier for reimbursement of benefits paid to a claimant while his workmen's compensation case was being litigated. (Section 15(8), 25, 206(2))

REVIEW ASSESSMENT - (A). An assessment made by the Board where the decision of a Referee is affirmed by the Board upon review. A carrier or employer seeking such a review is assessed $25; all other parties may be assessed $5. (Section 151)

S

SCHEDULE LOSS - (W,V). The number of weeks of compensation payable for permanent partial disability due to the loss or loss of use of certain members of the body or organs as listed in Section 15, Subd. 3 of the Law. (Section 10, V.F.B.L.)

SECOND INJURY FUND - (W). A Fund, technically known as the Special Disability Fund, created to encourage employers to hire physically handicapped persons by protecting them against a disproportionate liability in the event of subsequent employment injury. At the same time, the Second Injury Law assures the injured handicapped worker full workers' compensation benefits. (Section 15, Subd. 8)

SECOND INJURY LAW - (W). This Law is designed to encourage the employment of handicapped workers by limiting the liability of an employer in the event they sustain further permanent disability due to work-connected injury. (Section 15, Subd. 8) See also Second Injury Fund, above.

SELF-INSURANCE - (W,D,V). A method by which an employer or group of employers may secure the payment of workers' compensation or disability benefits to his or its employees by depositing securities or a surety bond in an amount required by the Chairman of the Workers' Compensation Board. This method is in lieu of purchasing insurance from an insurance company. (Sections 50, 211, W.C.L. and Section 3, Subd. 13, V.F.B.L.)

SICKNESS - (D). See "Injury".

SLOW-STARTING OCCUPATIONAL DISEASE - (W). The Law identifies the diseases in this category as those caused by compressed air illness or its sequelae, or by latent or delayed pathological bone, blood or lung changes or malignancies due to occupational exposure or contact with arsenic, benzol, beryllium, zirconium, cadmium, chrome, lead or fluorine or to exposure to X-rays, radium, ionizing radiation or radioactive substances. (Sections 28, 40)

SPECIAL FUNDS - (A). These are Funds specifically created in the Workers' Compensation and Disability Benefits Laws. There are ten such Funds. They are designed mainly to assure payment of benefits to claimants. In certain instances, (Section 15, Subd. 8, and Section 25-a) the liability of the employer for compensation to his injured worker is transferred to the Fund, and the employer is relieved in part or in whole of such liability. (Sections 15, Subd. 9, 25-b, 26-a, 107, 109-d, 214, 319)

SPECIAL FUNDS CONSERVATION COMMITTEE - (W). A committee created in accordance with Se'ction 15, Subd. 8 and Section 25-a of the Law to defend claims made against the Special Funds created under those sections.

SPECIAL FUND FOR DISABILITY BENEFITS - (D). Administered by the Chairman and used to pay benefits to (1) unemployed claimants whose disability commences more than four weeks following termination of employment; (2) employees of covered employers who have failed to comply with the requirement to have disability benefits insurance; and (3) employees of a covered employer whose insurance carrier fails to'pay the benefits. (Section 214)

STATE INSURANCE FUND - (A). A Fund created by the State pursuant to Section 76 of the Law for the purpose of insuring employers in the field of workmen's compensation, disability benefits and volunteer firemen's benefit insurance.

STATUTE OF LIMITATIONS - (A). Statutory enactments that prescribe the periods within which actions may be brought upon certain claims or within which certain rights may be enforced. Some of the statutes of limitations in the Workers' Compensation Law are:

Section 15, Subd. 8. In a Second Injury Law case, the employer or carrier must file notice of claim for reimbursement from the Special Disability Fund within 104 weeks after the date of disability or death, or in a reopened case, no later than the determination of permanency upon such reopening.

Section 18. Written notice of injury or death must be given to the employer within 30 days after the accident causing such injury. (Note: The Board may excuse the failure to do so on specified grounds.)

Section 23. An application for Board review must be made within 30 days after notice of the filing of the award or decision of the Referee. An appeal to the Appellate Division, Third Department, must be taken within 30 days after notice of the Board decision.

Section 25-a. An application for compensation may be made against the Reopened Cases Fund after a lapse of seven years from the date of injury or death and also a lapse of three years from the date of the last payment of compensation. Awards made against the Reopened Cases Fund are not retroactive for a period of more than two years immediately preceding the date of filing of the application for reopening.

Section 28. The right to claim compensation is barred unless a claim for compensation is filed with the Chairman of the Board within two years after the accident. An employer is deemed to have waived the bar of this statute unless the objection to the failure to file the claim within two years is raised at the first hearing on such claim at which all parties in interest are present. Also, no case in which an advance payment is made is barred by the failure to file a claim. (IMPORTANT: The Board may not excuse the failure to file a claim within the two-year period.)

Section 40. The time limitation between contraction of an occupational disease and disablement therefrom is 12 months, but such time limitation is inapplicable in the slow-starting diseases enumerated in the Law. It is also inapplicable in the case of an employee who has continued in the same employment with the same employer from the time of contracting the disease up to the time of his disablement thereby.

Section 54, Subd. 5. No contract of workers' compensation insurance may be cancelled within the time limits in such contract, prior to its expiration, until at least 10 days after notice of cancellation is filed in the office of the Chairman and also served on the employer.

Section 110. Every employer shall report within 10 days the occurrence of an accident resulting in personal injury which causes a loss of time beyond the day of the occurrence or which requires medical treatment beyond ordinary first aid or more than two medical treatments by a person rendering first aid.

Section 115. No limitation of time shall run as against any person who is mentally incompetent or a minor so long as he has no committee or guardian.

Section 123. No awards of compensation or death benefits may be made after a lapse of 18 years from the date of injury or death and a lapse of 8 years from the date of the last payment of compensation.

All sectional references are to the Workmen's Compensation Law unless otherwise indicated

Section 217. In a Disability Benefits Law case, notice of disability must be furnished to the employer within fifteen days; and proof of claim, within twenty days. Late filing of proof of claim does not invalidate claim - (See "Notice and Proof of Claim"). No benefits are payable unless proof of disability is furnished within twenty-six weeks after start of disability. In the case of an unemployed claimant, the disability must commence within 26 weeks following termination of employment. (Section 207)

STATUTORY BENEFITS - (D). Under the Disability Benefits Law, the statutory weekly benefit rate is 50% of the employee's average weekly wage; maximum $95.00 per week, minimum $20.00 per week or average weekly wage if latter is less than $20.00. Statutory disability benefits are payable, after a 7-day waiting period, for a maximum period of twenty-six weeks in any fifty-two consecutive weeks or during any one period of disability. (Section 204, Subd. 2, Section 205, Subd. 1)

STATUTORY COVERAGE - (D). The benefits specified in the Disability Benefits Law which an employer must provide for his employees unless the Board has approved an employer's plan which provides benefits which are different but at least as favorable as the statutory benefits. In the case of an existing obligated plan which was in existence prior to April 13, 1949, the benefits provided may be less than statutory. (Article 9)

STATUS QUO ANTE - (W,V). The term signifies that a claimant's health has returned to what it was before the occurrence of the accient.

SUBPOENA - (A). A legal writ commanding a designated person to appear and give testimony at a workmen's compensation hearing under penalty for failure to do so. The Chairman, Board Members, Referees, officers of the Board designated by the Chairman and any attorney may sign and issue a subpoena, or a subpoena duces tecum, the latter requiring the production of records. (Sections 119, 142(3), 231)

SUBROGATION - (A). The assignment of a cause of action against a third party by the claimant to the carrier. Failure of a claimant to commence a third party action, if cause therefor exists, within the period of time specified in Section 29 (in a Workmen's Compensation case) and 227 (in a Disability Benefits case) operates as an assignment of the cause of action to the carrier liable for the payment of compensation or disability benefits provided that proper notice of such subrogation is given to the claimant. (Sections 29, 227, W.C.L.; Section 20, V.F.B.L.)

T

TEMPORARY REDUCED EARNINGS RATE (TRE) - (W). A temporary reduced earnings rate of compensation pending adjudication of the actual amount of reduced earnings or the determination of the claimant's reduced wage earning capacity. (Section 15, Subds. 5, 5-a)

TENTATIVE RATE (TR) - (W). The tentative rate of compensation pending final adjudication of the issues relating to rate. (Sections 14, 15)

THIRD PARTY SETTLEMENT - (A). When an employee is injured by the negligence or wrong of a party he may sue such party other than the employer or a fellow employee, if injured in the course of employment. The carrier which has paid compensation or disability benefits to the employee has a lien against any recovery in the third party action. A settlement of such action is called a third party settlement. (Sections 29, 227, W.C.L.; Section 20, V.F.B.L.)

U

UNINSURED EMPLOYERS' FUND - (W). A special fund which provides for the payment of workmen's compensation in cases where the employer was not insured nor self-insured, and he has defaulted in the payment of workmen's compensation. (Section 26-a)

W

WAGE EXPECTANCY - (W). The wages of a claimant, who is a minor at the time of the occurrence of the accident, are presumed to increase under normal conditions, and the Board may consider that fact in establishing the claimant's compensation rate if his injuries are permanent. (Section 14, Subd. 5)

WAGES - (W,D). The money rate at which employment with an employer is recompensed under the contract of hiring with the employer and shall include the reasonable value of board, rent, housing, lodging or similar advantage received under the contract of hiring. (Section 2, Subd. 9, Section 201, Subd. 12)

WAITING PERIOD - (W,D). Neither workmen's compensation nor disability benefits are allowable for the first seven days of disability, except that (1) in the case of an on-the-job accident, if disability exceeds 14 days, cash compensation is allowable from the date of the disability; and (2) in the case of disability benefits, (a) the sick unemployed, receiving unemployment insurance at the time they become sick, are not subjected to a waiting period, and (b) under a plan or agreement accepted by the Chairman, the waiting period may be less than 7 days or eliminated entirely. There is no "waiting period" in V.F.B.L. cases. (Sections 12, 204, 2D7, 211)

www.ingramcontent.com/pod-product-compliance
Lightning Source LLC
Chambersburg PA
CBHW081813300426
44116CB00014B/2344